Solomon R. Guggenheim Museum, New York

Oskar Kokoschka 1886–1980

Publication made possible by United Technologies Corporation

6,000 paperback and 500 hardback copies of this catalogue have been printed for the Trustees of The Solomon R. Guggenheim Foundation on the occasion of the exhibition *Oskar Kokoschka 1886–1980* at the Solomon R. Guggenheim Museum, New York. 2,000 hardback copies have been printed for United Technologies Corporation.

Library of Congress Cataloging-in-Publication Data

Kokoschka, Oskar, 1886–
   Oskar Kokoschka, 1886–1980.

   Catalog of an exhibition held at the Solomon R. Guggenheim Museum, New York.
     Bibliography: p. 244
     1. Kokoschka, Oskar, 1886– —Exhibitions.
I. Calvocoressi, Richard.   II. Schulz, Katharina, Dr.
III. Solomon R. Guggenheim Museum.   IV. Title.
ND1329.K58A4   1986   759.2   86-24851
ISBN 0-89207-060-9
ISBN 0-89207-059-5 (pbk.)

Texts by Richard Calvocoressi and Katharina Schulz
Copyright © 1986 The Tate Gallery
Works by Oskar Kokoschka © Cosmopress, Geneva, and ADAGP, Paris 1986

Published by The Solomon R. Guggenheim Foundation, New York, 1986

Frontispiece: Kokoschka in 1970, photograph by Derry Moore

Art Director: Derek Birdsall RDI
Designer: Andrew Gossett

Typeset in Monophoto Poliphilus, 170 and *Blado italic*, 119 and printed in Great Britain by Balding + Mansell Limited on Parilux matt white

Photographic credits
Colour plates
Jörg P. Anders 5, 34   Beverly Hills, California, The Robert Gore Rifkind Collection 106   Beverly Hills, California, The Robert Gore Rifkind Foundation 29   Prudence Cuming Associates Ltd. 24, 27, 41, 64, 70, 81, 85, 87, 91, 92, 149, 174   Fotostudio Otto 37, 84   Vladimir Fyman 62, 96, 159   Eric Ed. Guignard 176   Marianne Gurley 6, 22   David Heald 30, 119, 124, 152   Colorfoto Hans Hinz 46, 103   Los Angeles County Museum of Art, The Robert Gore Rifkind Center for German Expressionist Studies 104   Marlborough Fine Art (London) Ltd. 126, 127, 140   Neue Galerie der Stadt Linz, Wolfgang-Gurlitt-Museum 2   New York, The Museum of Modern Art 8, 10, 25   New York, Serge Sabarsky Gallery 4, 7, 17, 43   Pittsburgh, The Carnegie Museum of Art 63   John Tennant 20   John Webb 14, 53, 55, 57, 60, 65–67, 75, 78, 80, 88, 89, 93, 94, 97, 98, 100, 111, 113–118, 129–131, 134, 135, 137, 155–158, 161–167, 169–171, 175, 179, 180–182   Werberstudio-Herbert Stecher 102

Black and white plates
Tate Gallery Photographic Department

Hugo Erfurth p. 226   Hamburg, Erika Fleer p. 243   London, *Daily Express* p. 241   Derry Moore p. 243   Munich, Sven Simon p. 242   Pöchlarn, Oskar-Kokoschka-Dokumentation pp. 222, 223, 225   Vienna, Bildarchiv der Österreichischen Nationalbibliothek pp. 218, 220, 231

Contents

We are pleased to be partners with the Guggenheim Museum in one of the most thorough surveys of paintings and drawings by a modern master of surpassing imagination and energy: Oskar Kokoschka.

We hope the Kokoschka show and this catalogue provide much pleasure.

Robert F. Daniell
President and Chief Executive Officer
United Technologies Corporation

Foreword and Acknowledgements

Oskar Kokoschka's name remains linked to his native Austria a hundred years after his birth but its bearer was nothing if not cosmopolitan. His horizons from an early age transcended national boundaries and his art today is a universal possession. Kokoschka's partially Czech derivation, his stylistic affinity with German Expressionism, his extensive travel and subsequent expatriation and the three citizenships he embraced during his politically eventful life are the visible marks of his pronounced internationalism. His polyvalence, however, was not merely of an ethnic and geographic kind, but was above all cultural and humanistic, deriving its strength and convictions from inheritances that his curious and alert mind absorbed from many civilizations while his painter's eye was nourished by the study and a reasoned absorption of a rich stylistic heritage. Freed by such inner wealth, Kokoschka could allow his senses to act as primary conveyors of information and knowledge, thereby attaining rather early in his life a high degree of originality.

For a wide museum public in the United States it would appear that Oskar Kokoschka is a name without great substance. This may well be due to the tradition that has closely linked the history of modern art with France, somewhat at the expense of a broader cultural awareness. Related to this is the long-time absence, at least from New York, of important Kokoschka surveys and the relatively sparse representation of Kokoschka's work in museum collections and on the art market. For all these reasons but also because of a marked increase in public response to Central European cultural stimuli, the time for a major Kokoschka presentation at the Guggenheim Museum seems ripe.

The current retrospective is based upon the Tate Gallery's exhibition *Oskar Kokoschka 1886–1980*, organized by Richard Calvocoressi, Assistant Keeper in the Tate's Modern Collection, whose concept and selection it follows. For various reasons deviations from the original presentation were significant enough to be recorded here in a revised and restructured version of the Tate Gallery's catalogue. Since the exhibition travelled from London to Zurich before coming to New York, more than a marginal number of works were recalled by lenders unwilling to be separated from their treasures for an extended time-span. To maintain the high qualitative level established by the organizers it was necessary to seek substitutions which were as closely equivalent as possible to the works that were withdrawn. In addition, the available spaces at the Guggenheim Museum were more restricted than those of the Tate Gallery, and reduction of the exhibition size, particularly in the area of drawings, was therefore indicated. Moreover, insofar as the Tate show addressed itself to an English public, according to New York standards it overemphasized Kokoschka's London period, and the resulting imbalance was redressed in collaboration with our English colleagues.

None of this could have been achieved without the generous attitude evidenced by Mr Calvocoressi and his collaborators or without the support of the Tate Gallery and Alan Bowness, its Director. We owe a profound debt to Olda Kokoschka, the artist's widow, for her enthusiastic and essential participation in this project. Gilbert Lloyd and the staff of Marlborough Fine Art, London, have been helpful throughout, and Johann Winkler in Vienna has provided us with valuable assistance. The lenders to the original version as well as those who made loans exclusively to the Guggenheim Museum are not only deserving of institutional gratitude but also have earned the appreciation of museum visitors who could not have enjoyed the exhibition without their generosity. Nor could the retrospective accompanied by a new catalogue have come to New York without the munificent sponsorship of United Technologies Corporation extended throughout the life of the exhibition. Lufthansa German Airlines has helped to reduce costs by contributing transatlantic shipments and the Austrian Institute through its director Peter Marboe also has made important efforts in our behalf. We are indebted to both. We finally would like to credit the Guggenheim's Susan B. Hirschfeld, Assistant Curator, for having most effectively assisted in the exhibition's restructuring, Carol Fuerstein, Editor, for having performed an analogous task relative to the revised version of the catalogue, and Thomas Padon, Curatorial Assistant.

Thomas M. Messer, Director
The Solomon R. Guggenheim Foundation

Lenders to the Exhibition

Albright-Knox Art Gallery, Buffalo, New York
Art Institute of Chicago
Cincinnati Art Museum
Detroit Institute of Arts
Harvard University Art Museums (Busch-Reisinger Museum)
Harvard University Art Museums (Fogg Art Museum)
Hirshhorn Museum and Sculpture Garden, Smithsonian Institution, Washington, D.C.
Historisches Museum, Vienna
Kunsthaus, Zurich
Kunstmuseum, Basel
Kunstmuseum, Winterthur
Los Angeles County Museum of Art, The Robert Gore Rifkind Center for German Expressionist Studies
Moderna Museet, Stockholm
Musée Jenisch, Vevey
Museum of Art, Carnegie Institute, Pittsburgh, Pennsylvania
Museum of Art, Rhode Island School of Design, Providence
Museum Boymans-van Beuningen, Rotterdam
Museum Folkwang, Essen
Museum of Fine Arts, Boston
Museum of Modern Art, New York
Museum Moderner Kunst, Vienna
Museum am Ostwall, Dortmund
Národní Galerie, Prague
National Museum of Wales, Cardiff
Neue Galerie der Stadt Linz, Wolfgang-Gurlitt-Museum
Österreichische Galerie, Vienna
Phillips Collection, Washington, D.C.
Saint Louis Art Museum
Scottish National Gallery of Modern Art, Edinburgh
Solomon R. Guggenheim Museum, New York
Sprengel Museum, Hannover
Staatliche Museen Preussischer Kulturbesitz, Nationalgalerie, Berlin

Staatsgalerie Stuttgart
Stedelijk Van Abbemuseum, Eindhoven
Szépművészeti Museum, Budapest
Tate Gallery, London
Wellesley College Museum
Wiener Städtische Wechselseitige Versicherungsanstalt

Lord Croft
Mr and Mrs Prescott N. Dunbar, New Orleans
Mrs W. Feilchenfeldt, Zurich
Walter Feilchenfeldt, Zurich
Willard B. Golovin, New York
The Duke of Hamilton
Italian Family Collection
Kniže Collection
Estate of Senta and Alfred Marnau
The Robert Gore Rifkind Foundation, Beverly Hills, California
Basil Trakman

Marlborough Gallery, Inc., New York, and Marlborough Fine Art (London) Ltd.
Galerie Pels-Leusden, W. Berlin
Serge Sabarsky Gallery, New York
Galerie St. Etienne, New York
Galerie Würthle, Vienna

Introduction *Richard Calvocoressi*

Vienna and Berlin 1908–16

The past decade and a half has witnessed an extraordinary interest in the cultural life of Vienna at the turn of the century, an interest which is not confined to the German- and English-speaking countries of the western world but which has spread to Italy and even France, culminating in a series of large, interdisciplinary exhibitions over the last two years in Venice, Vienna, Paris and most recently here in New York. If they were not previously household names, the people who contributed most to the late efflorescence of high culture under the Habsburgs have become so now: Klimt, Kokoschka and Schiele; Wagner, Hoffmann and Loos; Mahler and Schoenberg; Schnitzler and Musil; Freud, Wittgenstein and Kraus.

The picture of 'Vienna 1900' as a homogeneous group of artists and intellectuals, many of them from the liberal Jewish bourgeoisie, battling against a stolid establishment is largely a myth. Ideas certainly cross-fertilized but not everybody knew one another intimately. Within the avant-garde itself (if such a self-contained entity really existed) there were factions and animosities: that between Loos and Hoffmann, for example, or Kraus and Freud – or, for that matter, Kraus and practically everyone. Different ideals and values co-existed but more often clashed. The early Kokoschka, that is to say up to 1908, is best seen in the context of *Jugendstil*, a florid late-symbolist style similar to *art nouveau* which made a strong impact on the applied arts and which in painting is associated with the artists of the Vienna Secession. Like so many German and Austrian painters who were to develop in an expressionist direction, Kokoschka's background was in the applied arts. He studied at the School of Applied Arts and in 1907, while still a student, became an associate of the Wiener Werkstätte, the geometrizing design workshops run by the architect Josef Hoffmann. *The Dreaming Youths*, Kokoschka's proto-expressionist illustrated 'fairy-tale', which he dedicated to Klimt, was published by the Werkstätte in 1908. He also designed posters and postcards, and decorated fans for them. But by the summer of 1909, when he graduated from the School, his style and pre-occupations had begun to shift fundamentally. Encouraged by the architect Adolf Loos, who took

a paternal interest in him, the twenty-three-year-old Kokoschka severed his connection with the Werkstätte and exchanged a moderately secure job in commercial art for the financially uncertain world of the portrait painter. Although his subjects were some of the leading Viennese intellectuals of the day, especially the small circle of writers and musicians around Loos and Kraus, temperamentally he had left 'Vienna 1900' far behind; and within a year he had gone to seek his fortune in the more receptive, less provincial climate of Berlin.

The *fin-de-siècle* cult of decadence scarcely affected Kokoschka, although a powerful sense of physical and mental decline is evident in a number of his early portraits. But the morbid self-consciousness and concern with adolescent eroticism typical of the more mannered art of Egon Schiele are conspicuously absent. Kokoschka let violence and sexuality emerge in his poems and plays, notably *Murderer Hope of Women*, but in the final analysis they must count as *juvenilia*. In his paintings he concentrated less on giving a literal record of his sitters than on portraying their psychological traits. Factual likeness, though not to be ignored, was subservient to capturing the emotional mood or feel of his subject. In this respect Kokoschka differs substantially from his German Expressionist contemporaries – for instance Kirchner and the artists of *die Brücke* – in whose work the portrait plays a relatively minor role. The *Brücke* insistence on pure saturated colour and spontaneous brushstroke as signifying the primitive or elemental qualities they cultivated has no parallel in Kokoschka's work of this period. Colour is severely muted in the earliest portraits, which give the curious impression of being barely painted at all. As we might expect from someone who began his career as a graphic artist, line is used to great expressive effect.

Much has been written of Kokoschka's 'X-ray eyes', his ability to penetrate the minds and even the souls of his models. Kokoschka himself once used the memorable phrase 'a psychological tin-opener'[1] to describe his method of encouraging the sitter to move, talk, read or become absorbed in his or her thoughts, unconscious of the artist's presence, before he would start work. Most of the early portraits are half-lengths, usually stopping just below the hands, on which the artist places heavy emphasis. Fingers are shown clenched or clasped, as in the portraits of Loos (No. 5) and Harta (No. 6); unnaturally bent or distorted (Nos. 9, 12); or long and sensitive as in the majority of female portraits (Nos. 8, 9, 11, 12). Sometimes the hands are outlined or stained in red, an idea developed in portraits from 1911 onwards in subtle passages of flesh and earth tones which evoke the colour and texture of putrefying meat[2]. In the paintings of consumptives done in Switzerland in early 1910 (Nos. 11–14) this blood red is allowed to impregnate the face, giving ominous spots of high colour to an otherwise deathly pale complexion. Facial features may also be delineated in red, suggesting veins or blood vessels (No. 5). The spectator's attention is frequently drawn to the eyes, which are often asymmetrical, with one larger than the other (Nos. 4, 15). Their owners occasionally look directly at the spectator but more usually gaze distractedly elsewhere, as if obsessed with their own inner selves.

Whereas Schiele's figures communicate through an exaggerated body language, Kokoschka's portraits rely on minute inflexions of face and hands for their smouldering psychological charge. Bodies are seldom contorted but remain comparatively inert. In the portrait of Lotte Franzos (No. 9), for example, her body is indicated perfunctorily by a bluish aura drawn around it, while her clothes are almost completely unpainted, leaving visible large areas of ground. Such an insubstantial appearance lends a visionary quality to the image; this is intensified by the blank, anonymous background which isolates the subject even further. By contrast with their bodies, the sitters' faces and hands seem to twitch and pulsate with life. This can partly be explained by the peculiar manner in which they are painted. Kokoschka would often scratch the wet paint with the sharp end of the brush or possibly with a fingernail, producing lines of varying degrees of thinness which form a complex network of graphic signs at certain crucial points. Sometimes these lines animate the space around the figure, as in the portrait of Joseph de Montesquiou (No. 13), where they perform a decorative function perfectly suited to the doll-like, effeminate appearance of the sickly aristocrat. In Kokoschka's portrait drawings of 1910, such as 'Karl Kraus' (No. 107), 'Herwarth Walden' (No. 108) and 'Paul Scheerbart' (No. 109), every muscular and nervous tic is exposed on the surface of the skin, joining scars, warts, wrinkles and other

external blemishes in a vibrant pattern of marks and dots made with the pen, the equivalent of the brush handle or fingernail.

The paint texture of several early oils is thin and dry, with a rubbed or scraped quality that implies the use of the hands or a cloth. The effect of this flatness and lack of modelling is to convey an eerie sense of immediacy, as if a photographic negative or X-ray of the model had been imprinted on the canvas. A handful of pictures, such as the brightly coloured 'Still-life with Pineapple' 1909, and the portraits of Loos, Harta and 'Father Hirsch', employ thicker, oilier conglomerations of paint and a more energetic brushstroke, suggesting the influence of Van Gogh, whose work Kokoschka first saw at the international *Kunstschau* in Vienna in the early summer of 1909. Kokoschka's portraits share with Van Gogh's certain obvious characteristics, including a preference for half- or three-quarter-lengths seated against stark backgrounds and depicted full-face or half-turned; and a prominence given to the hands, which are shown either tense and gesticulating (Nos. 6, 7, 9), resting on a table or the back of a chair (No. 3), folded together (No. 5), or holding an object such as a book (No. 28). But above all it is the humanity and nervous intensity of Van Gogh's images which Kokoschka transposes into his own, idiosyncratic idiom. Whether he also knew Van Gogh's ink drawings, with their hatchings, loops, whorls and other rapid calligraphic strokes, is not recorded; but it seems likely in view of the foregoing.

Van Gogh apart, there seem to have been few influences on Kokoschka's style before 1911. An exception is the nineteenth-century Austrian artist Anton Romako (1832–1889), whose work was collected by Oskar Reichel, the father of the 'Boy with Raised Hand' (No. 15). Romako, who eventually committed suicide, was something of an 'outsider', a painter of large-scale historical scenes as well as more intimate portraits of neurotic-looking young society women, reminiscent of exotic plants in a greenhouse. Their bright staring eyes and rarefied manner may have had a direct bearing on Kokoschka's portrayal of the languid young Hans Reichel, to give an obvious example. But while Romako's art is in danger of crossing the border into stylized melodrama, Kokoschka never loses sight of his objective. In his hands the portrait becomes a deposit of human experience, rather like an archaeological site which the artist must excavate (Freud used a similar analogy to describe the psychoanalytical process). His early work is curiously homespun and styleless, a quality that would have appealed to Loos, with his cult of

Sachlichkeit and dislike of all things arty. One man's honesty, however, may be another's ugliness. There are accounts of Kokoschka's clients refusing to buy, or declining for years to hang, their portraits, on the grounds that they were cruel and 'unlike' themselves, or because they felt they had been made to look thirty years older. Equally, there are stories of a model growing to resemble his or her 'likeness' years afterwards.

It has been remarked that 'the artist is always tempted to invest his models with his own psycho-physical qualities.'[3] Kokoschka was no exception; in later years especially he would project his long upper lip and pugnacious chin on to the faces of his sitters, male or female, so that in extreme cases the finished result is closer to self-portraiture. The notion of empathy is crucial to an understanding of Kokoschka's sensibility: 'I cannot paint everybody. It is only people who are on my antennae . . . certain people whom I discovered an affinity with – with one facet of my own being.'[4] This may explain why, in the early portraits, we are rarely given any clues as to the social status, profession or interests of the person depicted. Paul Stefan, in the first monograph on Kokoschka published in 1913, laid great stress on the autobiographical element in his work, finding that 'the pictures of this period . . . express first of all the artist Kokoschka; they say what he was suffering then'.[5]

A less romantic view was put forward thirty years later by Edith Hoffmann, who recognized a collaborative as well as therapeutic process in Kokoschka's relationship with his sitters.

> *Once he had realised what the faces of his friends expressed, he was filled with fear for them; but at the same time was seized by an indomitable urge to relieve his own fears and uncertainties by fixing theirs on his canvas.*[6]

Certainly Kokoschka can lay claim to have painted the first existential images of alienated modern man, in which the individual is stripped of mask and pretence – or, to use his own word, 'opened'. Like the sculptor Rubek in Ibsen's *When we Dead Wake* (1899) he could truthfully say: 'What I turn out aren't just portraits . . . there's something subtle and equivocal lurking below the surface . . .'[7]

During 1911 a change gradually came over Kokoschka's painting, probably as a result of his recent contacts with the more cosmopolitan art world in Berlin, where he had lived for much of the previous year, helping Herwarth Walden on his Expressionist periodical *Der Sturm*. The change is noticeable in works of different

type. In portraiture, the subject is rendered with greater plasticity, almost equal attention being paid to the body as to the face and hands. Gone are the etiolated, semi-transparent forms of 1909–10, to be replaced by emphatically modelled volumes and a more mature sense of the possibilities of colour and brushwork. New structural concerns are evident in the series of paintings on biblical themes (No. 21), in which the figures are integrated with their environment by a dense all-over faceting. This softening of outline, which can likewise be seen in the portrait of Egon Wellesz (No. 20), is a striking departure from Kokoschka's earlier employment of a sharp contour to define physical mass. It recalls Cubism, as, too, does the general opacity of the 1911 pictures. In 1912, however, Kokoschka broke through to a sparkling translucency in paintings such as 'Two Nudes' (No. 23), 'Alpine Landscape, Mürren' and the portrait of Alma Mahler (No. 24). The pastel colours, particularly pink, blue, green and yellow, and the fragmented, crystalline structure of these works suggest the influence of a Cubist offshoot such as Robert Delaunay. In 'Two Nudes', an odd transitional picture in which the figures are not very satisfactorily opened up into surrounding space, Kokoschka seems to be attempting to express movement of a kind.

Delaunay's work would have been familiar to Kokoschka. Four of his pictures were included in the *Blaue Reiter* exhibition which toured Germany in the winter of 1911–12 and which Herwarth Walden incorporated in his first *Sturm* exhibition (in which Kokoschka was represented) at Berlin in March 1912. Walden showed Delaunay again in the second *Sturm* exhibition in April. Apart from his connection with Walden, Kokoschka had reasonably good relations with the *Blaue Reiter* through his friendship with Schoenberg. But there is a second, literary source which may conceivably account for Kokoschka's jewel-like style of 1912: the utopian architectural theories of Paul Scheerbart. Scheerbart was closely involved with *Der Sturm*; in 1910 Kokoschka painted his portrait (No. 17) and also drew him for the magazine (No. 109). Scheerbart's crystalline vision, which he had been refining since the 1890s, was finally published in *Der Sturm* in 1914. In it he speaks of a spiritual need to 'transform our architecture'.

> *. . . this will be possible only if we remove the enclosed quality from the spaces within which we live. This can be done only through the introduction of glass architecture that lets the sunlight and the light of the*

moon and stars into our rooms not merely through a few windows, but simultaneously through the greatest possible number of walls that are made entirely of glass–coloured glass.[8]

Finally, it is worth noting that Kokoschka, according to Edith Hoffmann, was experimenting with a prism at this time.[9]

Kokoschka's new-found painterliness was also in part a result of his engagement with older masters, to begin with El Greco, who was then being rediscovered in Germany. The figures in Kokoschka's small religious pictures probably derive from El Greco, their pale, drawn faces, elongated bodies and stylized hand gestures evoking a mystical dimension in keeping with the subject matter. In his portraits, with their frontality, austerity and, not least, dark, almost black backgrounds, Kokoschka reveals even more clearly his debt to El Greco, whom many years later he would recognize as 'an expressionist painter'.[10] He was also drawn to the heightened colours and dramatic illusionism of Franz Anton Maulbertsch (1724–96), the leading Austrian master of late Baroque, whose breathtaking ceiling frescoes in the Piaristenkirche in Vienna had made such a profound impression on him as a boy. In later years a baroque sense of space and movement became a hallmark of Kokoschka's style, as in 'The Prometheus Saga' triptych of 1950 (also a ceiling painting) where he may have been consciously recalling Maulbertsch. But his strongest admiration at this time was reserved for the Venetians, especially Titian and Tintoretto, whose work he saw on a visit to Venice with Alma Mahler in March 1913. The great symbolic compositions of 1913–14, in which Kokoschka either celebrates his love for Alma Mahler, reflects on its problems, or foretells the end of the relationship (Nos. 26, 27, 30 and 'The Tempest'), demonstrate a freer technique and an awareness of light as a means of enlivening surface and denoting depth. Paint is generally creamier and applied in broad, fluid strokes. Colour, though often restricted to a sombre range of blue and green or brown and grey tones, is rich and sensuous, while forms are highlighted with bold touches of white, sometimes flecked with red, causing the image to quiver before our eyes. The predominant effect is one of restless, dynamic movement. Furthermore, 'Still-life with Putto and Rabbit' and 'Knight Errant', despite their iconographic complexity, are self-allegories of haunting power: not until the Second World War would Kokoschka be roused to produce works of equal emotional intensity.

Dresden 1917–23

In January 1915, five months after the outbreak of war, Kokoschka volunteered for a cavalry regiment in the Austro-Hungarian army. Eight months later he was badly injured in the head and the lung during a skirmish with Russians on the eastern front. At the end of October he was brought back to Vienna, where he remained in hospital until February 1916 and where he convalesced for a further three months. The portrait of Heinrich von Neumann (No. 31), the doctor treating him, dates from this time. In July Kokoschka was posted south to the Italian front to serve as an officer responsible for looking after war artists and journalists. In late August he developed shell-shock and was transferred once again to a military hospital in Vienna. A week later he was released and given extended sick leave by the army.

By the end of the year, after a brief stay in Berlin, Kokoschka had been admitted to a sanatorium in the rural Weisser Hirsch district of Dresden. Here, at a nearby inn, he met a handful of pacifists, most of them Expressionist actors, playwrights or poets, who became his companions and whom he used as models in two symbolic group portraits, 'The Exiles' 1916–17 and 'The Friends' 1917–18. Other paintings of this period, such as 'Lovers with Cat' (No. 32) and 'Portrait of the Artist's Mother' 1917, demonstrate a feverishness in execution which may reflect the artist's precarious state of health. Scarred both physically and psychologically by his wartime experiences, Kokoschka was further depressed by the break-up of his affair with Alma Mahler. The trend towards greater naturalism discernible in the portraits of 1911–14 is now reversed. Paint is worked into a thick impasto by means of writhing, organic brushstrokes, so that at certain points the forms appear to loosen and even dissolve altogether.

'Lovers with Cat' is one of a handful of major oils, including 'The Tempest' 1913–14 and 'Woman in Blue' 1919, for which there are preliminary drawings in pencil or ink. Otherwise Kokoschka rarely made sketches in advance, with the exception of the occasional more ambitious or formal portrait, such as those of Masaryk (No. 63), Maisky (No. 73), and Kathleen, Countess of

Drogheda (No. 76), for which quite detailed studies exist. The early portraits, on the other hand, were all painted direct from the sitter.

If the paintings of 1917 present a degree of formal incoherence, those of 1918–19 onwards, beginning with 'The Power of Music' (No. 33), seem by comparison more compact and resolved. In terms of colour they relate to German Expressionism, for instance Nolde and some of the artists of the *Brücke*, whose work Kokoschka knew from his association with Herwarth Walden in Berlin before the war. The composition is now disposed in irregularly shaped smears and patches of pure unmixed colour – usually green and the primaries, especially red – which are not divided by contour lines but which abut one another directly. The effect is of a dazzling radiance akin to stained glass. Kokoschka himself was the first to recognize the monumental possibilities of his new language of colour. He had in fact been commissioned by the architect Max Berg to paint frescoes for a crematorium at Breslau shortly before the First World War; and, although the project was never realized, he remained interested in the problems of creating a cycle of large-scale images intended to be seen from a distance.[11]

'The Power of Music', 'Mother and Child' (No. 37) and 'The Slave Girl' (No. 40) are double-figure compositions with both sensual and violent overtones, suggesting that pathos and brooding introspection were still important elements in Kokoschka's work. The series of Dresden townscapes, however (Nos. 35, 38), strikes a lighter, more optimistic note. In the summer of 1919 Kokoschka was appointed to a professorship at the Dresden Academy, a job he had coveted ever since arriving in the city over two years previously. He moved into his studio in the academy, which overlooked the Elbe, in the autumn, and from its balcony painted the first of several views across the wide river with its elegant bridges. The baroque houses and spires huddled together on the opposite bank are translated by Kokoschka into a jostling patchwork of small planes and strips of colour. In one picture of the series, 'Dresden, the Elbe Bridges (with figure from behind)' 1923, the silhouette of his own head and shoulders dominates the foreground, turned away from the spectator in contemplation of the scene, while a yellow tram crosses the nearest bridge beneath which a barge floats silently by. Such details look forward to those atmospheric panoramas in which he would brilliantly convey the very essence of London, Prague and other centres of European culture and history which meant so much to him.

'Self-portrait with Doll' (No. 34), executed in the broad flat brushstrokes typical of this period, brings us to the strange episode of the life-size doll or puppet which Kokoschka had made in the image of Alma Mahler. Every detail of its construction, articulation and external appearance, down to the colour of the hair and soft texture of the 'skin', was closely supervised by the artist, who corresponded at length with the puppet-maker Hermine Moos between August 1918 and February 1919, when the creature was ready to be dispatched to its owner. Kokoschka's instructions were illustrated with anatomical drawings and diagrams; a selection of the letters was later published in an anthology under the title 'The Fetish' (1926). Stories of what the disillusioned Kokoschka did or did not do with his 'beloved' once it had arrived – some true, others wildly exaggerated – have been repeated ever since. What is certain is that he made over twenty drawings of the doll and used it as a model for the painting 'Woman in Blue', which, like 'The Power of Music', is built up of slabs of contrasting pigment.

There has been much speculation about Kokoschka's motives in ordering the doll. The artist's own version was that, after his first-hand experience of brutality and destruction, he could no longer tolerate humanity – a reaction to the war not uncommon among German artists if we consider the nervous breakdowns suffered by Max Beckmann and Ernst Ludwig Kirchner. But in Kokoschka's case the phobia extended only to man: throughout his life he preferred and sought out the company of women, whom he regarded as his protectors. A more likely theory is that the artist was determined to live up to the image of *der tolle Kokoschka*, 'crazy Kokoschka', a nickname conferred upon him in Dresden in 1918 but one which echoed the bewildered and sometimes hostile comments of the Viennese nearly a decade earlier. Whether genuine mental imbalance was also involved, we are not in a position to judge. Certainly by the time the artist left Dresden and set off on his travels in the summer of 1923, Kokoschka the nihilist – who had briefly been taken up by the Zurich Dadaists in 1917 – was a figure of the past.

Travels 1923–30

Given the worsening political and economic situation in Weimar Germany, it is not surprising that Kokoschka should have wished to leave Dresden. Furthermore, having gained recognition in Germany, his work was slowly becoming known internationally, and he was eager to consolidate his position. At the 1922 Venice Biennale he shared the German pavilion on an equal basis with the three giants of German Impressionism, Liebermann, Slevogt and Corinth. Throughout the next decade exhibitions of his work occurred with increasing frequency, not only in the principal German cities but also in Zurich, Amsterdam, London and Paris.

A summary of Kokoschka's movements between August 1923, when he left Dresden, and September 1930, when he came to roost in Paris, gives some idea of his astonishing energy and intense curiosity for new sights. During those seven years – that is, between the ages of thirty-seven and forty-four – he visited eleven different European countries (including Ireland and Scotland) and explored much of North Africa and the Middle East. His travels began in earnest in February 1925, when his agent, the famous Berlin art dealer Paul Cassirer, agreed to subsidize his trips on a generous scale in exchange for a regular supply of landscapes. Kokoschka was accompanied on these journeys by Jakob Goldschmidt, an associate of Cassirer's, who owned a gallery at Frankfurt. Goldschmidt's job was to take care of the hotel and travelling arrangements, make sure the artist had canvas, easel and paints, and dispatch the finished pictures to Berlin. After Cassirer's death in early 1926 Goldschmidt's place was taken by the more sympathetic Helmut Lütjens, who ran the Amsterdam branch of Cassirer's. Lütjens was Kokoschka's travelling companion on his visits to Italy, Switzerland and France in 1927, and to North Africa and Ireland in 1928, although he would return periodically to Amsterdam, leaving Kokoschka, who relied on him, feeling lonely. An art-historian who specialized in drawings, Lütjens treated his charge with tact and understanding, normally going on ahead of Kokoschka to select views for him to paint.

The dating of the so-called 'travel pictures' has been made easier by the survival of a succession of illustrated post-cards which Kokoschka sent to his family in Vienna and to other friends, sometimes at the rate of two or three a week. On the back of these cards he would invariably give a brief account of his progress, noting the start or completion of a painting, the state of the weather, his future plans and so on. In the case of the three Scottish landscapes of summer 1929 ('Scotland, Dulsie Bridge', 'Scotland, Plodda Falls' and 'Junction of the Divie and Findhorn Rivers'), he sent back picture post-cards showing the actual motif of each: whether the purchase of a particularly striking or attractive photograph inspired him to go and search out the original must remain a matter for conjecture. On this occasion there was no Lütjens to help him choose the most picturesque spots, although Walter Feilchenfeldt, one of Cassirer's successors in Berlin, brought Kokoschka to the north of Scotland and stayed with him there for a few days.

Whenever he could, Kokoschka preferred to look down on his motif from a high viewpoint, climbing to the top of a hill or the tenth floor of a building in order to achieve maximum breadth and distance. He also adopted the unusual technique of painting the same picture from two different standpoints, so that, as he later recalled, 'I doubled the width of my visual field'.[12] This double perspective accounts for the slightly spherical composition of many of his townscapes, similar to a wide-angle photograph, as well as the sense of a spinning motion that inhibits the eye from fixing on a single focal point and which gives equal significance to what happens at the periphery of vision. In short, they are at their best paintings which capture the very feel of life itself; even Kokoschka's buildings, it has been said, seem to 'grow, move and breathe'.[13]

In these paintings of the twenties Kokoschka fully lived up to the promise he had already shown as a landscape artist in 'Les Dents du Midi' of 1910, which so convincingly reproduces the invigorating sight of an ethereal alpine landscape under snow. In that work the sun is shown breaking through mist or cloud, a typically baroque effect which Kokoschka repeated in the twenties and which he continued to use up until the last landscapes of the 1960s, though his manner of suggesting light became more summary, almost ideographic. But the similarities with the earlier picture end there. To suit his new habit of painting in the open air or from hotel balconies, Kokoschka evolved a style radically different even from the works of the immediately preceding Dresden phase. In the latter, the spectator is made conscious of paint as *material*, as if it were a substance like clay which the artist has worried and moulded into thick slabs; colour breaks free from its descriptive function and assumes an autonomous role. If we compare this approach with a painting such as 'London, Tower Bridge' 1925, or 'The Coast at Dover' (No. 46), we notice both a stronger degree of objectivity in response to the subject matter and a corresponding relaxation in pictorial terms.

Instead of oil paint being applied straight from the tube, it is diluted with turpentine, allowing a swifter execution and resulting in a thinner, transparent surface closer to watercolour. Line reappears in Kokoschka's painting, though in an informal, sketchy manner which bears no relation to the hard contours and incisions of the early portraits: drawing and colour are now indistinguishable. There is nevertheless nothing hesitant about the brush marks, which are rapidly made and numerous. Every variegated touch contributes an essential note to the description of a scene in all its detail, and has its place in the composition. Objects such as buildings are foreshortened (but never gratuitously distorted), the more to give an illusion of deep space. The longest Kokoschka took to complete a landscape was about two weeks; the shortest, according to Edith Hoffmann, 'a day or two'.[14] In northern Europe he was frequently held up by bad weather – fog in London, pelting rain in Inverness-shire. He therefore needed to codify his myriad impressions as quickly as possible, before the light changed and conditions worsened. The scudding March skies of the two 1926 Thames views (Nos. 47, 48) are among the grandest he ever painted; while in 'Lyons' (No. 54), with its seagulls dipping and soaring overhead, we can almost feel the artist's presence, wrapped in a thick overcoat against the chilly December gusts.

Water clearly fascinated Kokoschka, nowhere more so than when the heart of a big city was bisected by a broad, mysterious river. In his autobiography he leaves us in no doubt that what attracted him to London was the Thames, 'that artery of life flowing from century to century'.[15] His excitement at seeing the metropolis for the first time is conveyed in the following post-card to his mother, written on 15 July 1925.

Within my first hour of reaching London I immediately found the right place to paint from. On the 10th floor of a building by the Thames. Below me the whole of the river and a city 10 times the size of Vienna.[16]

Towards the end of his ten-day stay he confided to a friend that

The country made a very strong impression on me, because it was my first experience of an Anglo-Saxon nation and I needed several days to get over my very great astonishment. And also because in the near future I shall be relying on these people and want to be accepted by them. I took it much more seriously than Paris, Madrid or Rome etc.[17]

The next year Kokoschka decided to return for longer, postponing plans to visit Egypt and Palestine. He intended to 'paint the 15–20 pictures I want to get done this year in England, on the coast, and in Scotland and Ireland'.[18] In the event he appears to have spent most of his time, from March to September 1926, in London; he did not travel to Ireland until 1928, and it was the summer of 1929 before he finally reached the Highlands of Scotland.

In addition to the Thames views, which were painted from the eighth floor of the Savoy Hotel, Kokoschka completed some half-dozen pictures during his stay in London, including a portrait of the dancer Adèle Astaire (No. 49), 'Richmond Terrace' and three animal subjects: the exotic 'Mandrill' (No. 50) and 'Tigon', both painted at Regent's Park Zoo, and a family of deer (No. 51) surprised in Richmond Park. Shortly after arriving he wrote a letter to his mother which expresses the touching mixture of awe and affection with which he regarded the English.

. . . here I am living on the 8th floor of the smartest hotel in Europe. You can imagine how inhibited I feel; I daren't even breathe, . . . Millions of people, hundreds of thousands of cars, my English useless, my memory gone to pot, my hearing defective; in other words, I feel like a stone on the street. I have to live this high up because from here I can paint the broadest vista of the Thames!

. . . I feel as apprehensive as a schoolboy, even though I'm so long in the tooth . . . We in Vienna are like negroes or savages by comparison with the real world of the English.[19]

By the spring of 1927 Kokoschka's financial situation had improved sufficiently for him to consider moving to England with his mother and younger brother, who were both dependent on him.[20] However, the idea, if it was ever very practicable, came to nothing. The following year the Leicester Galleries in London held a one-man exhibition of thirty-four paintings, his first ever in Britain. The catalogue carried a brief introduction by P.G. Konody, who took trouble to distinguish Kokoschka from the German Expressionists (who, he thought, were unlikely ever to be collected by the English) and gave a perceptive appraisal of the artist's most recent work. In spite of Konody's enthusiasm, however, the exhibition was not a success. T.W. Earp in *The New Statesman* described it as 'a salad compounded to a clever recipe . . . energy and virtuosity . . . singularly lacking in significance', although he did make an allowance for Kokoschka as a 'good, "straight" landscape' painter.[21] Kokoschka, who came to London for the opening, did not return to the city for another ten years, and then in very different circumstances.

Several commentators have attributed Kokoschka's years of *Wanderschaft* to his desire to create a modern version of the *Orbis Pictus*, a book which had made a lasting impact on him as a child.[22] In a long footnote to Edith Hoffmann's monograph, written during the dark days of the last war but not published until 1947, Kokoschka reaffirmed his belief in the importance of this illustrated encyclopaedia and the ideas of its author – the seventeenth-century Moravian theologian, pacifist and pedagogue Jan Amos Comenius – which seemed to him especially relevant now that the whole world was plunged into senseless conflict.

It pictured men of all nations as belonging to one family differing only in colour, language, religion, in their dwellings, habits, activities and sciences, and showed that these divisions were due to geography and climate. . . . Words inscribed beneath the pictures in several living and dead languages, made it easy to learn the meaning when you could see the things and knew them to be true.[23]

But there were other, more personal reasons behind Kokoschka's conscious decision to broaden his horizons, which originate in the crisis he suffered during the First World War. In an interview with the critic Andrew Forge in 1962 he recalled his feelings at that traumatic moment in his life.

And then I thought . . . if I ever come out of this rat-existence alive, I will paint landscapes, because I have seen so little of the world, so I want to see everywhere, I want to go everywhere where the roots of my culture, of my civilization, are which lead back to the Greek, the Latin: I must see all that.[24]

Despite his preoccupation with landscape in the twenties, Kokoschka did not neglect portraiture, but continued to produce good work. While staying with his family in Vienna he took the opportunity to paint his old friends Arnold Schoenberg (No. 43), in 1924, and Karl Kraus (No. 45) in 1925. Nothing is allowed to detract in either portrait from the image of the sensitive artist concentrating on his particular task – Schoenberg playing the cello, Kraus fingering a book with one hand and gesturing with the other, as if reciting. Fine examples of expressionist portraiture though they undoubtedly are, they nevertheless typify the same systematic, less intuitive approach to subject matter that characterizes Kokoschka's townscapes and landscapes. This becomes more evident later in the decade, with the portraits of Elza Temary (No. 52), the Marabout of Temacine (No. 55) and Marczell von Nemeš (No. 56), in each of which the figure is drawn in greater volume and depth than hitherto and occupies more of the canvas. If the degree of paraphrase is minimal in comparison with the 'psychological' portraits of 1909–11, it is made up for by the massiveness of the subject, whose physical presence seems all the more palpably real. As if to balance this naturalistic treatment of the human figure, Kokoschka introduces a narrative element, for example in the portrait of Adèle Astaire (No. 49), where background objects or symbols allude to the interests and profession, and by implication the personality, of the sitter. Over the next twenty years Kokoschka would increasingly resort to this traditional device, sometimes including a complete scene in the background.

Adèle Astaire and Elza Temary are both portrayed with their dogs. Kokoschka's insight into animal character is demonstrated by the magnificent paintings of a mandrill and a tigon mentioned above. Both were hung in his exhibition, significantly titled *Portraits by Oskar Kokoschka: Humans and Animals*, held at Cassirer's in February 1927, alongside the portraits of Kraus, Nancy Cunard (No. 44), Adèle Astaire and Elza Temary. Concerning the mandrill Kokoschka later wrote: 'As I painted him, I saw: this is a wild, isolated fellow, almost a mirror image of myself who wants to be alone.'[25]

Vienna and Prague 1931–8

For the first nine months of 1931 Kokoschka lived in Paris, a city whose reputation as the European capital of fine art he regarded with suspicion, if not disdain. Years later at Salzburg he would warn his students of the corrupting influence of the 'beauty industry', as he dubbed the School of Paris.[26] In March 1931, however, Paris did Kokoschka the peculiar honour of a one-man exhibition at the Galeries Georges Petit, which was actually a reduced version of his retrospective held at Mannheim earlier in the year. It was surprisingly well received, and for a while it must have looked to Kokoschka that he was poised on the brink of international acclaim. Simultaneously with the exhibition at Petit's, the Museum of Modern Art in New York organized a large survey of *German Painting and Sculpture*, in which Kokoschka was represented by four oils, including 'Woman with a Parrot' 1916 and 'Girl with Doll' (No. 39).

In Paris Kokoschka rented a studio above Augustus John, who later did much to help Austrian and German artists find refuge from the Nazis in England.[27] In the summer Kokoschka took over the house and studio of his friend the painter Jules Pascin, who had committed suicide. He also met and was photographed by Brassai. But in September 1931, his contract with Cassirer's having collapsed some months previously, he was forced for financial reasons to return once more to Vienna. He spent a further year in Paris, from March 1932 to May 1933, during which time he painted 'Self-portrait with Cap' (No. 60) and a number of other works. It was in Vienna, however, that his art discovered a new sense of purpose, which grew stronger as the decade progressed inexorably towards its dreadful conclusion.

In 1920 Kokoschka had managed to buy his parents a villa in the Liebhartstal, a pleasant district on the western outskirts of Vienna consisting of mainly wooden houses, surrounded by gardens, orchards and avenues of chestnut trees. It was to this peaceful environment that Kokoschka repaired in the autumn of 1931, in time for his mother's seventieth birthday (his father had died in 1923). Refreshed and stimulated by his surroundings, he made friends with a fifteen-year-old girl, the daughter of a neighbour, who

agreed to pose for him. In all, some twenty drawings and half dozen paintings of Trudl exist, showing her in a variety of roles and moods (Nos. 58, 61, 155, 156). In their heavy, rounded forms and air of classical repose, these pictures are the direct antithesis of the portraits of highly strung individuals whose psyches he had probed, with an astonishing indifference to matters of technical skill, over twenty years earlier. If nothing else, a work such as 'Trudl with Head of Athena' 1931, with its range of sensuous reds, is a splendidly bravura piece of painting.

Chance played its part in turning Kokoschka's attention again to questions of content. Shortly after his arrival he was commissioned by the socialist council of 'Red Vienna' to paint a picture for a prominent place in the Town Hall. For a suitable theme he looked no further than his immediate neighbourhood. The Liebhartstal lies between two hills, the Galitzinberg and the Wilhelminenberg. Five minutes walk uphill from the Kokoschkas' house stood Schloss Wilhelminenberg, a former imperial palace which had been expropriated by the authorities and converted into an orphanage. Kokoschka was moved and encouraged by this development and, as he could hear and see the children from his second-floor studio window playing in the palace grounds, he decided to paint them.

'Vienna, View from the Wilhelminenberg' (No. 59) is a townscape with a difference. Although the background affords a panoramic view of the whole city, in which distant landmarks such as the spire of the nineteenth-century gothic Town Hall are clearly visible, the focus of the composition rests in the foreground activity. In the park beneath the palace little knots and clusters of children are shown playing specific games. Kokoschka based this idea on a famous painting by Brueghel in the Kunsthistoriches Museum. Somehow he must have connected it in his mind with his hero Comenius and the latter's ideal (as Kokoschka himself later put it) of 'the education of people to reason on the basis of using their five senses',[28] since each of the children's games in the picture – blind man's buff, ring-a-ring-a-roses and so on – involves the use of a different sense. Kokoschka argued that received opinion, second-hand knowledge, hearsay, or whatever we like to call it, was largely responsible for society's ills. To support his case he quoted St Thomas Aquinas: 'The senses are a kind of reason. Taste, touch and smell, hearing and seeing, are not merely a means to sensation, enjoyable or otherwise, but they are also a means to knowledge – and are, indeed, your only actual means to knowledge . . .'[29] This may explain why, after the war, he called his course at Salzburg the School of Seeing.

'Wilhelminenberg', then, is a symbolical painting. Given the high value Kokoschka attached to a supra-national constructive education, as opposed to military or nationalistic indoctrination, it is not difficult to understand why he later referred to it as his 'first picture with a political meaning'.[30]

Kokoschka's mother died in July 1934. Two months later, finding the political developments in Austria intolerable and disappointed by the lack of portrait commissions, Kokoschka departed for Prague. The four years he spent there were, in terms of his art, productive ones, but they were spoiled by the increasingly unstable international situation and by uncertainty about his own future. An outspoken opponent of Hitler, Kokoschka had published in a German newspaper an open letter in support of Max Liebermann after the latter, on account of his Jewish blood, was forced to resign as President of the Prussian Academy in May 1933. Furthermore, Kokoschka's pictures were beginning to be confiscated by the Nazis from German museums as examples of 'cultural Bolshevism'. But however grim the events in Germany, he was relieved to be away from the 'oppressive little world' of Vienna:[31] even when the city finally got round to giving him a retrospective in 1937 he refused to go back for it, and would never live there again. At least in Prague there was freedom of speech and a cosmopolitan atmosphere which appealed to him. He respected the people and their civilized traditions; and he fell in love with the city, which he painted more times than any other.

In the summer of 1935 Kokoschka took as his studio a turret in the roof of a tall nineteenth-century building on the banks of the Moldau, which gave him a spectacular view of the medieval Charles Bridge and the Hradschin castle on its hill opposite. It was in Prague that Kokoschka met Olda Palkovská, a young law student who was soon sharing his eccentric life and who later proved indispensable in helping the artist leave Czechoslovakia.

The two masterpieces of Kokoschka's Prague period, the first of which can be read as a political testimony, are the portrait of Thomas G. Masaryk (No. 63) and the ironically titled 'Portrait of a "Degenerate Artist"' 1937. The permission to paint the first President of the Czechoslovak Republic may have arrived before Kokoschka left Vienna. He instinctively warmed to this eighty-five-year-old democrat; their conversations ranged widely but tended to concentrate on Masaryk's humane educational policies, which coincided with and reinforced Kokoschka's own half-formulated ideas. Their mutual admiration for Comenius was a frequent topic of discussion. In the portrait, Kokoschka explicitly links Masaryk with Comenius, who is shown by the President's side holding up a tract, his *Via Lucis*, on which are illustrated the five sensory organs. Three months after starting work on the portrait Kokoschka said in an interview:

> . . . *According to Comenius it is easier to teach by means of pictures than by means of words; and so a modern, symbolic portrait like this should serve to be instructive . . . Neither cape nor crown, neither sceptre nor sword, denote this President's status . . . I want to make it a historical picture; a picture that can be shown in schools, to teach the children that patriotic tasks, as well as personal duties are united in humanism.*[32]

The 'Portrait of a "Degenerate Artist"', even more than the portrait of Masaryk, concludes the switch to a monumental plastic style first intimated in Kokoschka's paintings of the mid-twenties but not fully evolved until the 'Trudl' series. Not the least remarkable aspect of this searching self-portrait is Kokoschka's brushwork, the superficial untidiness and spontaneity of which conceals a deft, assured touch which unites all the disparate elements of form, colour and tone into a resonant whole.

While working on the painting, Kokoschka heard the news from Germany that eight of his pictures had been included in the Nazis' notorious exhibition of *Degenerate 'Art'* at Munich. His immediate response was to alter the position of his arms so that they crossed in an attitude of defiance. At the end of the year he wrote to Edith Hoffmann in London, mentioning

> *A New Self-Portrait . . . suggestive and very good . . . it could be called 'Self-Portrait of a Pilloried Artist'. But it looks as if I'll have the last laugh at those fools' expense.*[33]

England 1938–46

In October 1938, less than three weeks after the Munich agreement which sealed the fate of that 'far-away country' Czechoslovakia, Kokoschka and Olda Palkovská managed to fly to London. Kokoschka entered the country on a Czech passport, Masaryk having helped him apply for Czech citizenship in 1935 – a step which was later to prove beneficial to the artist. In the panic of summer 1940, after the fall of France, thousands of German and Austrian refugees were classified by Parliament as 'enemy aliens' and interned. Czechs, on the other hand, were deemed to be 'friendly aliens', with a government in exile in London headed by Edvard Beneš; and although their movements about Britain were restricted, they were otherwise more or less left in peace. Kokoschka was thus in a good position to agitate for the release of his anti-Nazi and Jewish friends, including artists, from internment camps, and indeed for the repeal of the enemy alien law altogether. This was in line with the policies of the Free Austrian Movement and the Free German League of Culture, two refugee organizations in which he took an active part. In December 1941 Kokoschka called for an end to the 'scandal' of internment, which he denounced as 'the skeleton in the wardrobe of democracy', and for internees to be allowed to contribute to the war effort, especially since the Soviet Union had now joined the fight against Hitler and the opening of a Second Front seemed a possibility.[34]

Despite the setback of 1928, when his one-man exhibition at the Leicester Galleries attracted disappointing notices, Kokoschka's attitude towards England had remained positive. 'I like the English so much, as if they were my relatives', he wrote to Anna Kallin from Prague in February 1936.[35] His admiration, however, was soon tempered by understandable feelings of bitterness at the politics of appeasement and of mounting tension as war approached. Apart from anxiety about his own and Olda's personal future, he still had close relatives in Vienna and Prague (as did she). During the first nine months of the war he became progressively more depressed by what he identified as a growing hostility to foreign refugees, encouraged by a xenophobic English press, among people he had always associated with high standards of toleration. Nevertheless, as he wrote to Philip Moysey, his first English 'pupil', in the early summer of 1940, he was 'still optimistic as an artist to believe more in the good in man and not in the evil'.[36] Nor would he allow himself to feel an exile in Britain, or indeed in any country that was still free and part of European civilization. He was, after all, used to travelling light, and neither he nor Olda were sentimentally attached to particular countries or cities.

German-speaking readers of *The Spectator* in March 1936, shortly after Kokoschka's fiftieth birthday, would have found him praised as 'the most important German painter since the death of Liebermann'[37] – a judgement with which few English critics felt able to concur when nineteen of Kokoschka's works, including the 'Portrait of a "Degenerate Artist"' and 'Herwarth Walden' were shown in the exhibition of *20th century German Art* two years later at the New Burlington Galleries in London. Kokoschka himself had strong reservations about this exhibition, which was conceived as a gesture of moral, and, it was to be hoped, financial support for artists who were being ostracized by Hitler's barbarous cultural policies. To many people, however, it only confirmed their prejudice against German art. Even Liebermann was compared unfavourably to the French Impressionists.

A few weeks before the outbreak of war Kokoschka and Olda Palkovská left London, which was becoming too expensive for them, and went to live in the picturesque fishing village of Polperro on the southern coast of Cornwall, where the sculptor Uli Nimptsch and his family had settled. In a letter to the painter Hilde Goldschmidt Kokoschka described Polperro as a 'beautiful, healthy place ... much lovelier than a cosy little Italian port because so much more real' (*viel echter*).[38] His opinion was evidently not shared by the writer Rayner Heppenstall, who recounts a visit to Kokoschka in his autobiographical novel *Saturnine* (1943), the dustjacket of which Kokoschka illustrated.

Never had I seen a place so female, so closely shut in as this inhabited cleft between two plump hills, opening out at the front into a harbour over which one felt that hands were crossed in modesty. As a place to inhabit in the ordinary way, it was horrible.

I bore left along the crease between the right buttock and thigh, a little above the level at which this mighty, inverted limb plunges into the water.[39]

However ironical, the author succeeds in this extract in catching the intrinsically dramatic quality of the Polperro landscape, which alters with every step, revealing a succession of new shapes and vistas, both natural and man-made but all worn by centuries of fierce storms. Some of Kokoschka's finest wartime landscapes are in fact views of small fishing ports on the Atlantic coast of Britain. In addition to the series of Polperro oils and watercolours (Nos. 162–7), which were painted from the terrace of his cottage, he made coloured pencil sketches of Nevin in North Wales, Port William in south-west Scotland, and the less enclosed harbour of Ullapool on the north-west Scottish coast, where he also painted the oil 'Ullapool' (No. 75). Heppenstall's landscape-body analogy is not inappropriate to Kokoschka's work. While his cityscapes have been likened to living human profiles marked by time, so his landscapes occasionally seem to suggest an anthropomorphic element. Kokoschka himself wrote in his autobiography that 'All landscapes are given their shape by man; without a human vision no one can know what the world really is'.[40]

By the summer of 1940 it was no longer permitted to foreigners, friendly or otherwise, to remain in coastal areas, especially if they were close to important naval bases (Polperro is near Plymouth). Regulations had already come into force about photographing, sketching or painting sites designated as 'restricted', for which a written permit had to be obtained from the highest authority. In retrospect we may be grateful for these restrictions, since they forced Kokoschka to turn his mind to a medium, watercolour, which he had hardly touched since the 1920s. Back in London in September 1940, with the Blitz just beginning, he produced the first of many fresh and delicate still-lifes of cut flowers, thereby maintaining a symbolic link with nature until he was able once again to go out into the real landscape.

This became possible a year later, when he and Olda, by then married, were invited to stay with friends near Port William in Wigtownshire. It was the first of half a dozen visits over the next five summers (and one spring) to this remote region of lowland Scotland, with its stony, rather flat moorland dotted with sheep and cattle. In 1944 and 1945 they also went further north to Ullapool, which in peacetime had been a thriving centre of the herring industry but which was now a restricted area where convoys were assembled and commandos trained. Here they discovered some of the most spectacular scenery in the British Isles.

In London, much of Kokoschka's time was taken up with political activity, making speeches, writing articles for anti-Nazi refugee newspapers, and helping to raise funds. His abhorrence of nationalism, coupled with his own unique personal history – born an Austrian, regarded by many as a major German artist, but holding Czech citizenship – made him the ideal figure to bestride the various refugee political organizations, who tended to keep to themselves when they did not openly squabble. But his role was far from being merely symbolic. He threw himself into the campaign for an independent and democratic Austria after the war, an objective recognized by the Allies at the Moscow conference in 1943, and he became involved in the activities of Young Austria, the youth section of the Free Austrian Movement. During Austro-Soviet Friendship week in June 1942, Young Austria collected a large proportion of the £3,600 needed to buy two mobile X-ray units for the Red Army. The following year Kokoschka donated the £1,000 he received for his portrait of Maisky, the Soviet Ambassador (No. 73), to the Stalingrad Hospital Fund, idealistically stipulating that it be used to treat both the Russian and German wounded. When his portrait of Masaryk was sold in New York in 1944, he set up a fund for the war orphans of Czechoslovakia with the proceeds, at a time when he could ill afford to be so generous. In 1946 he was still trying to raise money for humanitarian causes – in this case 'for the Viennese children who are starving'. In an open letter to the critic Alfred Neumayer published in the American *Magazine of Art*, he declared his intention to find £1,000 in the U.S.A.

for a political painting I did in 1943, with the title: What We are Fighting For. *It is a large and striking work. If you know somebody or some institution interested in it I would like to send you a photograph of it . . .*[41]

'What we are fighting for' was actually the last, and certainly the most sardonic, in a series of five pictures attacking the war and the conduct of both axis and allied powers, which Kokoschka painted between 1940 and 1943 (Nos. 69, 70, 71, 72, 74). The experience of meeting and painting Masaryk in Prague had deepened and enriched Kokoschka's art to a degree that became explicit only now, when he felt an even stronger urge to clarify his intellectual and moral position. He resorted once again to a kind of baroque allegory, but he also drew on a specifically English tradition, that of political caricature, with its crowded figure compositions, discrepancies of scale, violent and grotesque imagery, animal and food symbolism, use of inscriptions and so on. Robert Radford has suggested that Kokoschka may have based 'The Red Egg' (No. 69) on Gillray's satire 'The Plumb-pudding in Danger' 1805, which shows Pitt and Napoleon greedily carving up the globe.[42] That Kokoschka was familiar with early nineteenth-century English political cartoons is confirmed by the fact that he sent Michael Croft an inscribed copy of F.D. Klingender's *Russia – Britain's Ally: 1812–1942* for Christmas in 1942. The book carried an introduction by the Soviet Ambassador Maisky, who was sitting to Kokoschka at the time; in it he pointed to certain obvious parallels between Napoleon in 1812 and Hitler in 1942. There followed an essay by Klingender and over fifty reproductions of popular caricatures by English and Russian artists past and present. Kokoschka knew Klingender, a Marxist art-historian who organized an exhibition of *Hogarth and English Caricature* under the auspices of the A.I.A. (Artists International Association) in the summer of 1943.[43] It is interesting to note that Bosch and Brueghel were cited in the catalogue as important influences on Hogarth; Edith Hoffmann, in her discussion of the anti-war pictures, specifically compares 'What we are fighting for' to 'works . . . of Kokoschka's admired master Brueghel'.[44]

The sarcastic political allegories represent a brief but intense phase in which Kokoschka perceived his art as having a didactic function. At one point in 1941 he was anxious to produce 'The Red Egg' in poster form, as emerges from a letter to Michael Croft.

Some friends of mine help together so that I can now print my Mussolini – Hitler caricature 'Appeasement' in colours and original size . . . And I will be the first one to have started a Red-cross help for it [the Red Army] *in selling my print for the benefit of the fighters.*[45]

How effective 'The Red Egg' would have looked translated into the flatter medium of lithography is open to doubt. Kokoschka's agitated brushwork, which vitalizes the image and conveys the artist's strength of emotion, would certainly have suffered; and the clashing, high-key colours, so finely judged in the original, might have seemed cheap and vulgar. But Kokoschka clearly wanted to reach a wider public. His chance came in 1945, when he found the money to print his drawing of a baroque Christ, based on a statue on the Charles Bridge by Matthias Braun, leaning down from the cross to comfort a group of children (p. 236). Along the crossbeam are inscribed the words 'IN MEMORY of the CHILDREN of EUROPE WHO HAVE to DIE OF COLD and HUNGER this XMAS.' Over a thousand (some say as many as 5,000) copies of this simple, moving image were put up in the London Underground and on the buses in December 1945. At an earlier stage Kokoschka seems to have been under the impression that it would be 'posted everywhere in England by the Church'.[46] For the artist, the significance of the poster lay in the fact that, as he wrote to Emil Korner, 'there is no organization, nor Party, nor collect mentioned'.[47] His art never descended to the level of ideological propaganda.

The loose, nervous handling of the political paintings is also apparent in the few portraits Kokoschka painted at this time, among which those of the young Michael Croft, his sister Rosemary (Nos. 66, 67) and Lady Drogheda (No. 76) are outstanding. In the two Croft pictures Kokoschka paints skin almost as if it were raw flesh, anticipating his own searing self-portrait of 1948 (No. 81) and the even more livid complexions of some later subjects. Rayner Heppenstall was the first to observe the deliberately allusive character of these new works.

. . . the background contains figures, landscape and symbolical images. Kokoschka will never do a portrait of anybody whom he dislikes or to whom he is indifferent. In the case of strangers to whom he may have taken a fancy, he will ask for photographs of their parents and themselves and will not begin work until he feels that he understands their history. Childhood scenes and faces of parents are likely to appear in the finished portrait.[48]

Switzerland 1947–74

Although the Kokoschkas did not finally settle at Villeneuve, on the eastern shore of Lake Geneva, until September 1953, from the spring of 1947, when Oskar's first post-war retrospective opened at Basel, they were almost continually on the move throughout continental Europe. In 1949 Kokoschka flew to the U.S.A. for the first time, to see the big travelling exhibition of his work there and also to teach at the Tanglewood Summer School near Boston, which in retrospect can be seen as the prototype of his School of Seeing at Salzburg.

As the war neared its end, Kokoschka's mood, instead of growing more optimistic, had darkened. He and Olda were concerned about the fate of their relations in Vienna and Prague, of whom there was no news. When word finally arrived, it was not promising: 'Prague is very bare of all food and clothing'; 'Vienna... seems to be worse off than any other part of the continent, no food at all and no contact possible'.[49] Their energies were devoted to writing, making enquiries and sending parcels of food, medicine and clothing by circuitous routes. On an international level, the allied bombing of Dresden, partly in order to please Stalin, appalled Kokoschka, as did the dropping of the first atomic bomb on the Japanese, an event he spurned as 'the logical conclusion of a mathematical attitude towards social problems'.[50] The future of eastern Europe seemed to him unutterably bleak: '... they drive wholesale men, women, old and young, babies and sick ones out from the countries with no land where to go. Millions of people die on the road'.[51] He was particularly worried about his sister in Prague, whom he succeeded in visiting in 1946 on the death of her husband. Over three million German-speaking Czechs had recently been expelled from the country, which within two years was under firm communist control.

Kokoschka's letter to Alfred Neumayer, published in 1946, is typical of several in which he expressed feelings of disillusionment and despair.

... the kind of world I would like to return to, my world in which I travelled as a happy tramp, does not exist any longer. Big towns have disappeared from the surface of the earth, great countries left as deserts. There is no end yet even of the murdering, which now goes on in a cold systematic way, no less inhuman than the murdering with weapons and machinery. Power politics extended the hunger-blockade after the 'cease fire'. To the destruction of cultural documents (of my home town, Vienna, only shabby remains tell of its former glory) the annihilation of humanistic values is connected in a way that makes seem normal today the callous views towards human life which we despised in Fascism... What Hitler sowed is ripening. His insane mind conceived the idea of the collective guilt, and, unfortunately, the post-war world sticks to this delusion of a madman, dispensing justice on such conceptions. I cannot live in such a world![52]

However, the exhibition at Basel in 1947 marked a turning-point. Its huge success gave Kokoschka back his 'joie de vivre, faith in humanity, and hope for the future', as he told his sister.[53] Kokoschka was now sixty-one and had just become a British subject. Over the remaining twenty-five years or so of his creative life he emerged as a public figure – to some a prophet – who spoke out against the dehumanizing effect of mass society wherever he detected it, in art as much as politics. Social engineering, belief in technological progress and, not least, standardized patterns of thought were evils which would lead to the 'suicide of society'. At Salzburg where he taught every summer from 1953 to 1963 he was at last able to put his anti-rationalist philosophy of learning through seeing – his language of the eye – to the test. Confronted by the rising tide of what he pointedly referred to as 'non-objective' art, he alone reiterated the importance of content and of the dynamic representation of space and light in painting. Respect for tradition, for the inheritance of Greece and Rome, became an integral part of his credo. In the great monumental works of the early 1950s, 'The Prometheus Saga' and 'Thermopylae' triptychs, he understood his mission as one of defending 'the artistic tradition of Europe'.[54]

Kokoschka continued to paint portraits. Beginning in 1949 with Theodor Körner, Mayor of Vienna and later President of Austria, his subjects included many of the architects of post-war European reconstruction. His townscapes became ever more atmospheric and broken in style, the best of them, such as 'Berlin, 13 August 1966' and 'New York' (No. 86), evoking a cosmic or apocalyptic dimension. As its relationship to ecstatic baroque rhythms grew more explicit, the visionary power of Kokoschka's painting intensified. In December 1953, shortly before starting work on the 'Thermopylae' triptych, he advised Philip Moysey to copy Rubens's 'The Judgement of Paris' in the National Gallery, London.

You ought to learn about the different ways of his wonderful brush, how he paints light, skin, complexion, the grey half-tones beneath the overlaying lustre and last touches. Sometimes he started with a tempera-white design, always used a reddish flesh-tone background, different layers, which you only can see, adore and get drunken with . . . when you are trying to copy it.[55]

In their robustness and vitality, the pictures on classical and mythological themes, such as 'Herodotus' (No. 84) or the massive 'Theseus and Antiope' (No. 93), rank with the grandest and most ambitious of Kokoschka's earlier works. The bright, powdery colours (especially scarlet and yellow), the vigorous and direct paint handling, and, after he had passed his eightieth birthday, the poignant, self-mocking images of the artist as an old man — all the hallmarks of a distinctive late style are present, comparable to Picasso's in its freedom and reckless disregard of academic norms.

Interviewing Kokoschka at the time of his Tate Gallery retrospective in 1962, Andrew Forge put it to the artist that 'the total sum of your work is like a painting of the whole world, as though you had tried to embrace the whole world, its cities, its people, its condition'.[56] The key to Kokoschka's *Weltanschauung* is best provided by those who sat to him or were taught by him. Gitta Wallerstein (No. 36) recalled that 'While he was working he was a lover towards his subject — both men and women . . .'[57] Philip Moysey and Ishbel McWhirter both remember him as an intuitive teacher who recommended them to ignore irrelevant prosaic detail and concentrate on the essentials of a person or scene. 'You have eyes, use them, love what you see', he told Moysey.[58] The word 'love' also occurs in Kokoschka's letters to McWhirter.

My advice is to portray as sincerely and well [as] you can do it — again and again! It will ease the tension and make you more human as an artist because love is the best teacher.[59]

It may sound trite or sentimental to talk about an artist's compassion, but there is no doubt that emotion, and not intellectual theory, was the basis of Kokoschka's teaching as it was of his art. His interest in children was informed by precisely similar feelings. As a student at the School of Applied Arts in Vienna he had fallen under the spell of the remarkable Franz Cizek, the pioneer of children's art education, who encouraged his classes to draw freely from their imagination as opposed to making sterile academic copies. Cizek was one of the first to take child art seriously; a room of his pupils' work was included in the 1908 *Kunstschau*, at which Kokoschka exhibited his illustrated 'fairy-tale' *The Dreaming Youths*. When Kokoschka was employed as a drawing master at Eugenie Schwarzwald's progressive school in 1911–12, he adopted Cizek's methods. His reading of Comenius, as we have seen, convinced him of the necessity of allowing a child to develop naturally through first-hand experience of the world, helped by pictures, demonstrations, games and other visual and practical aids. In London during the war Kokoschka opened two exhibitions of children's art, at which he outlined the educational ideas of both Cizek and Comenius. The second of these, *The War as Seen by Children*, was organized by the Refugee Children's Evacuation Fund, of which the educationalist A.S. Neill was a patron. Drawings by Neill's pupils at Summerhill were exhibited at the Arcade Gallery in London in 1944; and in April 1945 Kokoschka spent three weeks at another famous progressive school, Dartington Hall in Devon.

The School of Seeing, in other words, was the culmination of a lifelong concern with the true purpose and value of education. In 1941 Kokoschka wrote that 'The main task of democracy is to realize the universal debt of the old men to the youth of the world'.[60] At the School of Seeing he discharged that debt and inspired a whole generation.

Works on Paper

The earliest drawings in this exhibition (Nos. 94–101) date from Kokoschka's student years at the School of Applied Arts in Vienna (1905–9), in the latter part of which he also taught drawing to an evening class. In contrast to the conventional life-class, in which students were instructed to make detailed pencil studies of nude models who would pose motionless for long periods, Kokoschka introduced the practice of rapidly drawing figures in motion. For this purpose he would often use as his models circus children and urchins found playing in the street. Years later at Salzburg, where he founded his own School of Seeing in 1953, he resurrected this idea of drawing from the moving model, encouraging his pupils to capture the living, transitory moment: the 'feel' of a subject was more important than an inventory of his or her distinguishing marks.

Portrait drawings account for a large number of works on paper shown here, beginning with the magnificent series of heads which appeared in Herwarth Walden's periodical *Der Sturm* from 1910 onwards (Nos. 107–9). Kokoschka's turbulent relationship with Alma Mahler is immortalized in the drawings which he made for his lithographic cycles *Columbus in Chains* (No. 128) and *Bach Cantata* (Nos. 130, 131), in addition to the numerous sketches of places visited by the couple on their journeys through Italy. In 1916 Kokoschka served briefly as a war artist on the Italian front, where he produced pastel studies of gun batteries, trenches and a church damaged by shellfire, which are unusual in his work for their documentary accuracy.

Apart from this small group, there are few pastel drawings in Kokoschka's graphic oeuvre; his preferred medium seems to have been crayon. During the last war he began using coloured pencils for sketching outdoors. He later advised one of his pupils to keep a wallet of such pencils in her pocket but not to worry unduly which colour she selected. Another pupil remembers being allowed to graduate from pencil to coloured pencil, and only then to watercolour.

Certainly watercolour was another medium at which Kokoschka excelled, whether in the free expressionist figure studies of the 1920s, which are painted direct without preliminary pencil drawing (Nos. 148, 149, 153); the atmospheric views of Polperro harbour done in 1939 (Nos. 162–7); or the joyful flower pieces dating from the last years of the artist's career (No. 184).

Scottish and Welsh Sketches

Between September 1941 and September 1945 Kokoschka made a total of seven journeys to the Scottish and Welsh coasts, staying near Port William (Wigtownshire), at Ullapool (Ross-shire) and Nevin (Caernarvonshire). These trips gave Kokoschka the opportunity to rest, forget the war and renew his contact with nature. In addition to the assured and spirited watercolours of wild flowers, fruit, vegetables, fish, seafood and game (Nos. 168–70, 174, 175, 179), he started to draw with ordinary coloured pencils, filling up innumerable sketchbooks and drawing blocks with quick, shorthand notations which succinctly convey the essential structure of a motif. Taken together these sketches constitute a pictorial diary of his life in Scotland and Wales: people, animals, buildings, boats, vegetation, climate are all duly recorded. Looking through them we come across occasional studies for oils – for example, 'Scottish Coast' 1941, 'Scottish Landscape with Sheep' 1944–5 and 'Ullapool' (No. 75). Although Kokoschka painted in the open air, on a portable easel, when bad weather interrupted him he would finish the picture indoors, with his drawings serving as an aide-mémoire.

Notes

1 'Oskar Kokoschka Looks Back: A conversation with Andrew Forge', *The Listener*, 20 September 1962, p. 245.

2 From the beginning, critics have compared the 'disgusting' colours in Kokoschka's depiction of skin to those of Grünewald in the Isenheim Altarpiece. See, most recently, Alfred Werner, 'Kokoschka at Ninety', *American Artist*, April 1976, p. 35.

3 By Herbert Furst in *Portrait Painting, its Nature and Function*, London 1927, p. 139.

4 Conversation with Andrew Forge, p. 425 (see note 1 above).

5 Paul Stefan (intro.), *Oskar Kokoschka, Dramen und Bilder*, Leipzig 1913; quoted after Frank Whitford, *Oskar Kokoschka, a Life*, London 1986, p. 78. Stefan was one of the first to compare Kokoschka's portraits to caricature: '. . . he could not see people, only animals and spirits. And for him the human face became a caricature . . .'

6 Edith Hoffmann, *Kokoschka, Life and Work*, London 1947, p. 103.

7 Henrik Ibsen, *Ghosts and Other Plays*, Harmondsworth 1964, p. 228 (translated by Peter Watts). This comparison was suggested by Professor Ernst Gombrich.

8 Ulrich Conrads (ed.), *Programmes and manifestoes on 20th century architecture*, London 1970, p. 32.

9 Hoffmann, *op. cit.*, p. 115.

10 In a letter dated 24 November 1949 to a (Mr?) Kania (Kokoschka Archive, Villeneuve). In all fairness, Kokoschka distances himself in this letter from the modern cult of El Greco.

11 Kokoschka refers to the project in the interview with Andrew Forge (see note 1 above): 'And so I thought the colour must be large enough to reach people 200 yards away, or more; it must carry. So I had to study colour; the effect of light, and the harmonies of colours.' (p. 427). See also J.P. Hodin, *Oskar Kokoschka, the Artist and his Time*, London 1966, pp. 109, 165.

12 Oskar Kokoschka, *My Life*, London 1974, p. 123.

13 Hoffmann, p. 189.

14 *Ibid.*, p. 178.

15 *My Life*, p. 129.

16 *Oskar Kokoschka, Briefe II, 1919–1934*, edited by Olda Kokoschka and Heinz Spielmann, Düsseldorf 1985, p. 137 (translated by Anthony Vivis).

17 *Ibid.*, p. 138; letter to Marguerite Loeb (translated by Anthony Vivis).

18 *Ibid.*, p. 151; letter to Romana Kokoschka.

19 *Ibid.*, pp. 152–3 (translated by Anthony Vivis).

20 *Ibid.*, p. 158; letter to Anna Kallin.

21 T.W. Earp 'Fog and Fireworks', *The New Statesman*, 23 June 1928, p. 358. Walter Bayes was even more derogatory, singling out Konody's introduction for particular scorn ('Imports and Exports in the Arts', *The Saturday Review*, 23 June 1928, pp. 802–3).

22 See, for example, Hoffmann, p. 178; Peter Selz, *German Expressionist Painting*, Berkeley and Los Angeles, 1974 edition, p. 253; Hodin, *op. cit.*, p. 171. Kokoschka himself said he 'wanted to interest the onlooker, like a book . . . He ought to discover new little things here and there. His eyes ought to be led on a promenade through the picture' (Conversation with Forge, p. 427).

23 Hoffmann, p. 25.

24 Conversation with Forge, p. 426.

25 Quoted after Whitford, *op. cit.*, p. 149.

26 In a post-card to Ishbel McWhirter postmarked 10 September 1948 Kokoschka referred to the Ecole de Paris, 'where even the fashion dressers give up and settle for mass-production in New York. Paris is bankrupt just as French painting'.

27 John also supported the Young Austria movement in Britain: see correspondence in the Archives of the Austrian Resistance, Vienna.

28 'How I See Myself', *Oskar Kokoschka: early drawings and watercolours*, London 1985, p. 24; originally published in German as 'Der Bürgerschreck Kokoschka', *Die neue Weltbuhne*, Prague, 12 March 1936, pp. 335–9.

29 See note 23 above.

30 Hoffmann, p. 197.

31 Letter to F.K. Gotsch, 1 November 1934 (Kokoschka Archive, Villeneuve).

32 *Prager Tagblatt*, 8 September 1935 (translated by Anthony Vivis).

33 Letter to Edith Hoffmann, 24 November 1937 (Kokoschka Archive, Villeneuve).

34 *Zeitspiegel*, anti-Nazi weekly, 22 December 1941, p. 3.

35 Letter to Anna Kallin, early February 1936 (copy in Kokoschka Archive, Villeneuve).

36 Letter to Philip Moysey, June(?) 1940 (copy in Tate Gallery Archive).

37 F.G., 'Oskar Kokoschka', *The Spectator*, 20 March 1936, p. 513.

38 Letter to Hilde Goldschmidt, 30 August 1939 (Kokoschka Archive, Villeneuve).

39 Rayner Heppenstall, *Saturnine*, London 1943, p. 124.

40 *My Life*, p. 167.

41 'A Letter from Oskar Kokoschka', *Magazine of Art*, May 1946, p. 196.

42 Robert Radford, 'Kokoschka's Political Painting in Britain', typescript of an unpublished lecture, 1983, p. 4.

43 Kokoschka mentioned his admiration for Hogarth to Michael Croft in November–December 1938, while painting his portrait.

44 Hoffmann, p. 237.

45 Letter to the Hon. Michael Croft, late 1941.

46 Note to Emil Korner written on the back of a related sketch for Kokoschka's Christmas card, 1945 (repr. p. 237 here).

47 *Ibid.*

48 Heppenstal, *op. cit.*, pp. 127–8.

49 Letters from Olda Kokoschka to Constance Mitford, 6 June and 2 August 1945 (copies in Tate Gallery Archive).

50 Letter to Philip Moysey, 30 August 1945 (copy in Tate Gallery Archive).

51 *Ibid.*

52 See note 41 above.

53 Letter to Berta Patocková, 31 March 1947 (Kokoschka Archive, Villeneuve).

54 Translations of Kokoschka's explanatory texts on the two triptychs are published in Hodin, *op. cit.*, pp. 190–3.

55 Letter to Philip Moysey, 20 December 1953 (copy in Tate Gallery Archive).

56 *Loc. cit.*, p. 426.

57 Gitta Wallerstein's reminiscences are to be found in Hodin, pp. 155–9.

58 Philip Moysey, 'An account of my meeting with OK', unpublished typescript, 1985 (copy in Tate Gallery Archive).

59 Postcard to Ishbel McWhirter, 20 May 1949 (copy in Tate Gallery Archive).

60 'Children's Art Exhibition', *Oskar Kokoschka, Politische Äusserungen. Das schriftliche Werk*, vol. IV, edited by Heinz Spielmann, Hamburg 1976, p. 211. In the same speech, Kokoschka refers to Cizek as 'an old teacher of mine' (p. 209).

Vienna and Berlin 1908–16

1   *Hungarian Landscape 1908*

2
Father Hirsch
1909

3
The Court Tailor
E. Ebenstein 1909

4   *Martha Hirsch 1909*

5　*Adolf Loos 1909*

6   *Felix Albrecht Harta 1909*

7   *Peter Altenberg 1909*

8 *Dr Emma Veronika Sanders 1909*

9   *Lotte Franzos 1909*

10   *Hans Tietze and Erica Tietze-Conrat 1909*

11   *Bessie Bruce 1910*

12   *Victoria de Montesquiou-Fezensač 1910*

13   *Joseph de Montesquiou-Fezensač 1910*

14　*Conte Verona 1910*

15
Boy with Raised Hand
(Hans Reichel) 1910

16 *Herwarth Walden 1910*

17 *Paul Scheerbart 1910*

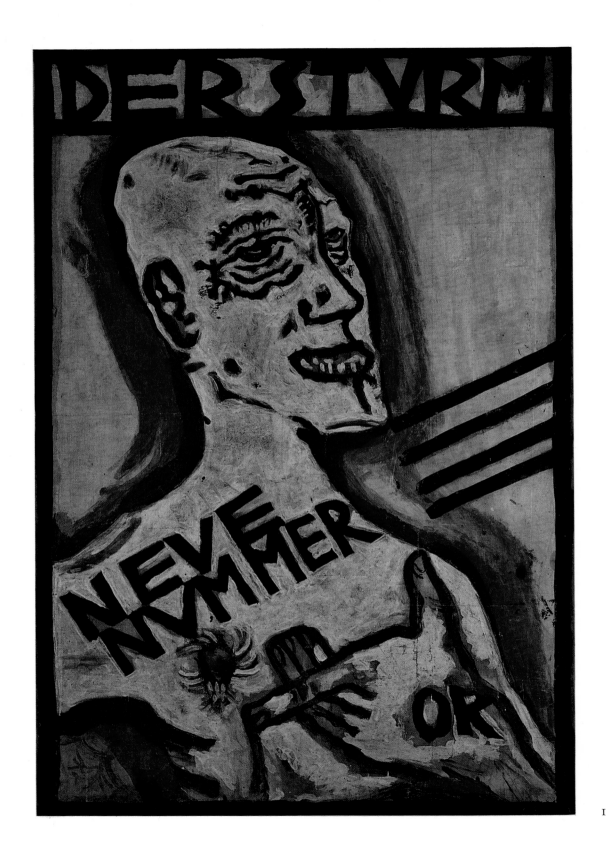

18   *Design for 'Sturm' Poster 1910*

19   *Else Kupfer 1911*

20   *Egon Wellesz 1911*   21   *The Annunciation 1911*

22   *Portrait of Mrs Karpeles 1911*

23   *Two Nudes 1912*

24 *Alma Mahler 1912*

25 *Self-portrait 1913*

26   *Two Nudes (the Lovers) 1913*

27   *Still-life with Putto and Rabbit 1914*

28   *Franz Hauer 1914*

29   *Emil Löwenbach 1914*

30   *Knight Errant 1914–15*

31   *Heinrich von Neumann 1916*

Dresden 1917–23

32   *Lovers with Cat 1917*

33 *The Power of Music 1918–19*

34   *Self-portrait with Doll 1920—1*

35 *Dresden, Neustadt II 1921*

36   *Gitta Wallerstein 1921*

37   *Mother and Child (embracing)* 1921

38   *Dresden, Neustadt IV 1921*

39
Girl with Doll
1921–2

40   *The Slave Girl* 1923

41   *Girl with Flowers 1923*

Travels 1923–30

42   *Lac Léman I 1923*

43 *Arnold Schoenberg 1924*

44   *Nancy Cunard 1924*

45 *Karl Kraus II 1925*

46   *The Coast at Dover 1926*

47   *London, large Thames View I 1926*

48   *London, Waterloo Bridge 1926*

49 *Adèle Astaire 1926*

50 *Mandrill 1926*

51　*Deer 1926*

52　*Elza Temary 1926–7*

53   *Fritz Wolff-Kniže 1927*

54 *Lyons 1927*

55   *The Marabout of Temacine (Sidi Ahmet Ben Tidjani) 1928*

56   *Marczell von Nemeš 1928*

57   *Arab Women and Child 1929*

Vienna and Prague 1931–8

58   *Pan (Trudl with Goat) 1931*

59   *Vienna, View from the Wilhelminenberg 1931*

60   *Self-portrait with Cap 1932*

61   *Mother and Child (Trudl with Noh Mask) 1934*

62   *Prague, View from the Villa Kramář 1934–5*

63   *Thomas G. Masaryk 1935–6*

64   *Olda Palkovská 1935–7*

England 1938–46

65   *Prague, Nostalgia 1938*

66
Michael Croft 1938–9

67
Posy Croft 1939

68   *Summer II (Zrání) 1938–40*

69   *The Red Egg 1940–1*

70   *Anschluss – Alice in Wonderland 1942*

71 *Loreley 1941–2*

72 *Marianne-Maquis 1942*

73   *Ivan Maisky 1942–3*

74   *What we are fighting for 1943*

75   *Ullapool 1945*

76   *Kathleen, Countess of Drogheda 1944–6*   77   *Acrobat's Family 1946*

Switzerland 1947–74

78   *Matterhorn I 1947*

79   *Werner Reinhart 1947*

80   *Venice, Santa Maria della Salute III 1948*

81   *Self-portrait (Fiesole) 1948*

82   *Cardinal dalla Costa 1948*

83   *The Feilchenfeldt Brothers 1952*

84   *Herodotus 1960–4*

85   *The Rejected Lover 1966*

86   *New York, Manhattan with the Empire State Building 1966*

87　*Morning and Evening (The Power of Music II) 1966*

88   *Self-portrait 1969*

89   *Agatha Christie 1969*

90   *The Duke and Duchess of Hamilton 1969*

91
Time, Gentlemen Please 1971–2

92 *Peer Gynt* 1973

93 *Theseus and Antiope* 1958/74

Works on Paper

94   *Standing Nude Boy* c.1906

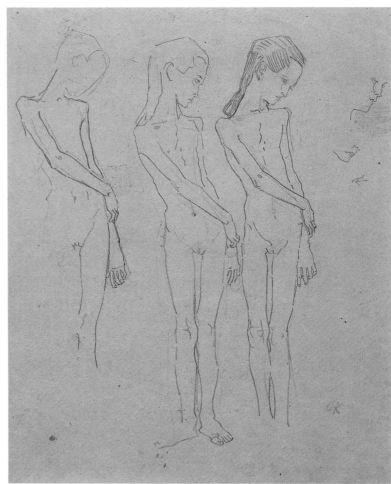

95   *Study for* The Dreaming Youths *1907*   96   *Three Studies of Nude Girl* c.*1907*

97 *The Acrobat's Daughter* c.1907

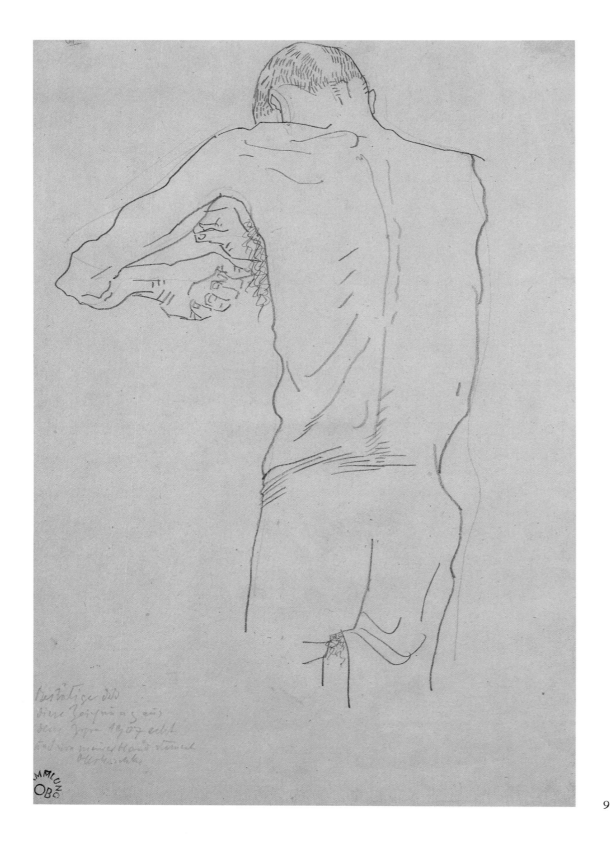

98 *The Acrobat* c.1907

99   *Nude with Back Turned* c.1907

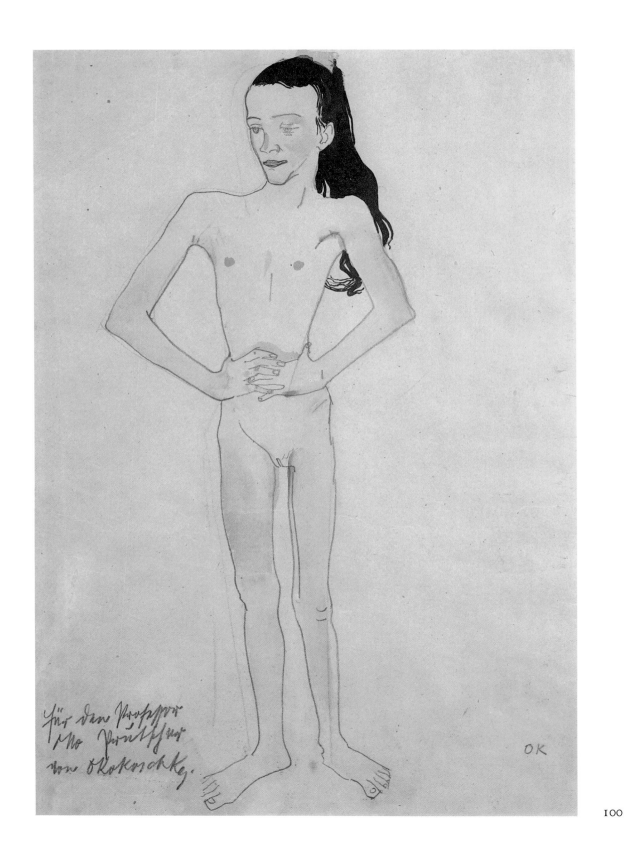

100   *Standing Nude Girl* c.1907–8

101   *Two Girls (trying on clothes)* c.1907–8

102 *Japanese Fisherman 1908*   103 *Storm at Sea 1908*

104   *Murder of a Woman, Illustration to*
Murderer Hope of Women *1908–9*

105   *Illustration to* Murderer Hope of Women *1910*

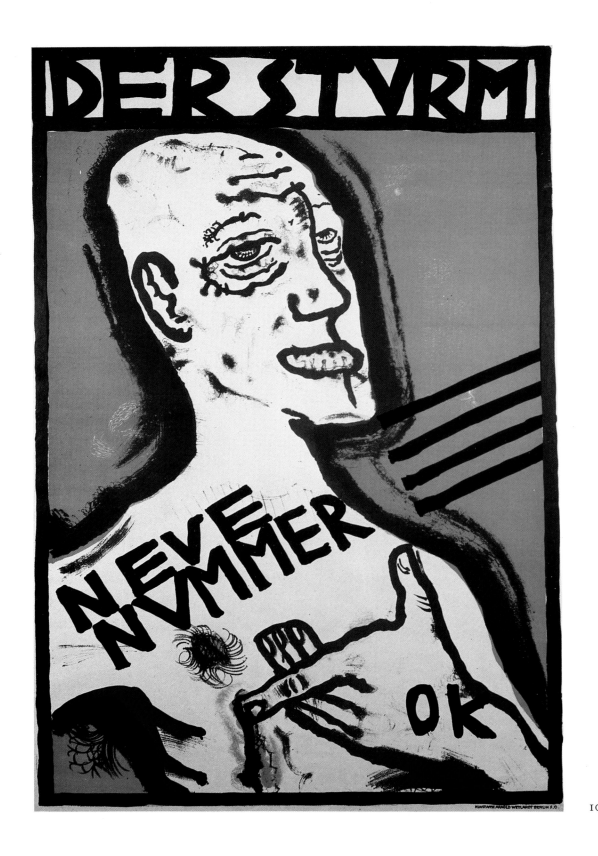

106 *Self-portrait* ('Sturm' *Poster*) *1910*

107   *Karl Kraus I 1910*

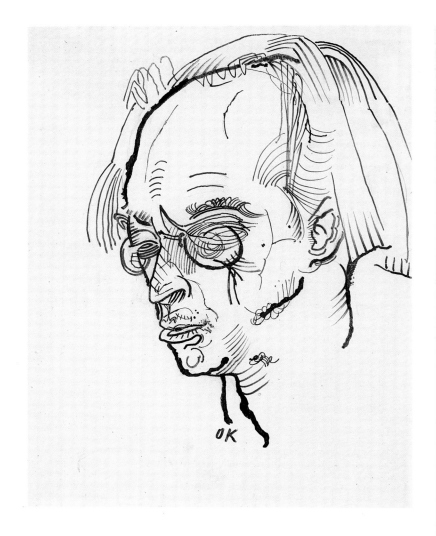

108   *Herwarth Walden 1910*   109   *Paul Scheerbart 1910*

110   *Lotte Franzos* c.*1911*   111   *Dr Fanina W. Halle* c.*1911*

OK

112 *Standing Nude* c.1911

113   *Standing Nude* c.*1911*

114   *Reclining Nude* c.1911

115   *Sleeping Nude* c.1911

116   *Seated Nude with Raised Arm* c.1911

117   *Seated Woman* c.1911–12

118   *Reclining Woman Leaning on Elbow* c.*1911–12*

119 *Reclining Woman* c.1911–12

120
The Savoyard Boy (half-length) c.1912

121
The Savoyard Boy (reclining) c.1912

am 12. April 1912 OK

122   *Alma Mahler 1912*

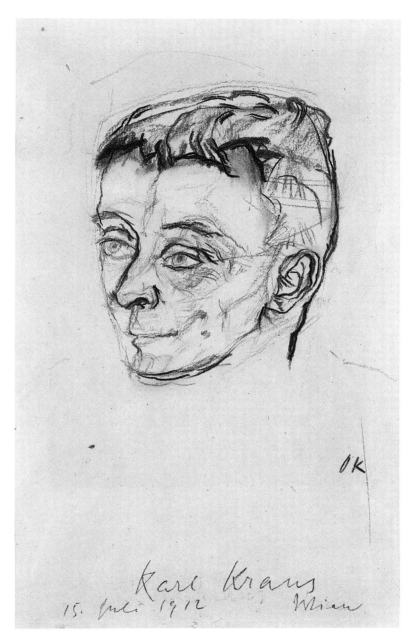

123 *Karl Kraus II 1912*   124 *Wilhelm Köhler 1912*

125   *Alma Mahler 1913*

126   *Crouching Nude 1913*

127   *Young Woman Reclining on Her Elbow 1913*

128 *The Meeting 1913*

129   *Tre Croci 1913*

130   *Study for* Bach Cantata *1914*

131 *Study for* Bach Cantata *1914*

132　*Portrait of a Lady 1916*

133   *Portrait of a Lady 1916*

OK 13. II. 1916

134   *Adolf Loos 1916*

135　*Rudolf Blümner 1916*　　　　　　　　136　*Hugo Erfurth 1916*

137   *Crucifixion 1917*

138   *Standing Girl* c.1919

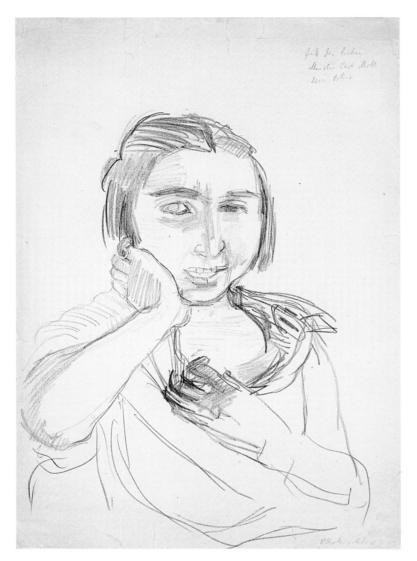

139   *Portrait of a Woman* c.1920–2   140   *Portrait of Ruth Landshoff 1920*

141 *Study for* The Concert *1920*

142   *Self-portrait 1920*

143   *Hugo Erfurth 1921*   144   *Hugo Erfurth 1921*

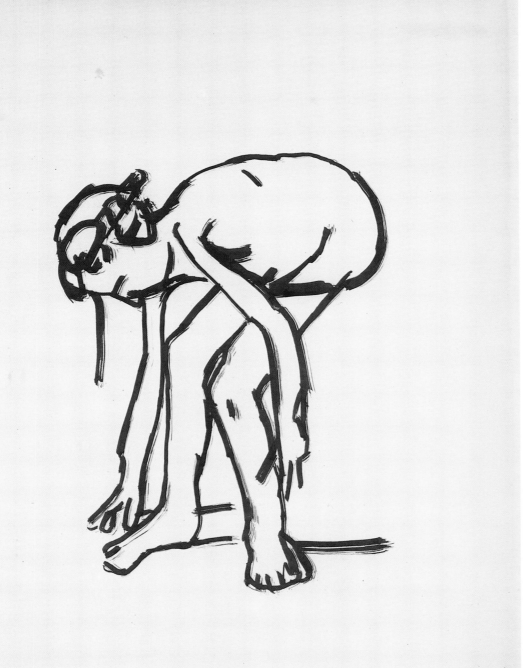

145   *Bending Girl* c.1921

146   *Girl Resting on Elbows* c.1921

147   *Seated Girl 1921*

148   *Seated Woman 1921*

149   *Fatne Khalil* c.*1921*

150 *Portrait of a Lady* c.*1921*

151   *Portrait of a Child* c.*1921*

152   *Reclining Nude* c.1923

153   *Oriental Girl with Jug 1923*

154   *Circus* c.1927

155 *Trudl 1931*   156 *Trudl with Arms Stretching Forward 1931*

157
Study for 'Thomas G. Masaryk' 1935

158　Olda 1935

159　F. Garcia Lorca 1936

160
Self-portrait 1936

161
Olda with Crown of Flowers 1938

162   *Polperro I 1939*

163　*Polperro II 1939*

164   *Polperro III 1939*

165 *Polperro IV 1939*

166 *Polperro V 1939*

167   *Polperro VI 1939*

168   *Summer Flowers, Elrig 1941*

169   *Mushrooms 1942*

170   *Fish 1942*

171   *Study for 'Ivan Maisky' 1942*   172   *Study for 'Ivan Maisky' 1942*

173   *Study for 'Scottish Coast' 1941*

174   *Duck Shoot 1943*

175 *Dead Pheasant 1944*

176
Study for 'Kathleen,
Countess of Drogheda' 1944

177   *Doris with Cat I 1945*   178   *Doris with Cat II 1945*

179   *Lobster 1946*

180   *Study for 'Matterhorn I' 1947*

181　*Mary Magdalene 1953*

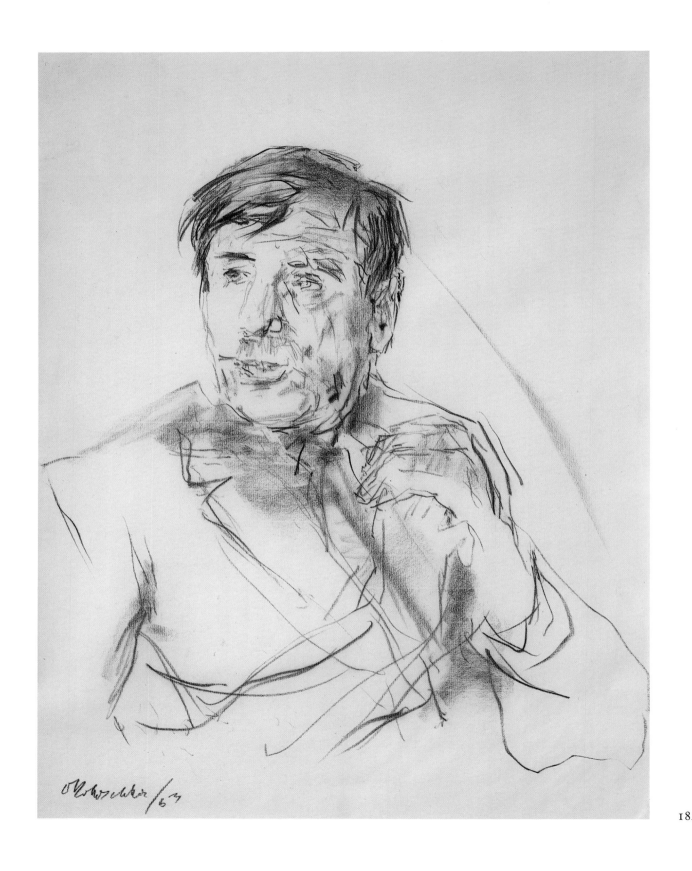

182   *Michael Tippett 1963*

183   *Self-portrait 1964*

184　*Irises 1972*

Catalogue

Dimensions are in centimetres and inches, height before width.

* Indicates not in exhibition.

Abbreviations
Hoffmann 1947
    Edith Hoffmann, *Kokoschka, Life and Work*,
    London 1947
Wingler 1958
    Hans Maria Wingler, *Oskar Kokoschka, The*
    Work of the Painter, Salzburg and London 1958

Sources
The principal source for the redating and retitling of Kokoschka's oils, particularly up to 1913 is the forthcoming catalogue raisonné by Johann Winkler (a revised and updated version of Wingler 1958). The dating of Kokoschka's early drawings is in a far less definitive state, not helped by the artist's occasional practice of inscribing dates years later, e.g. when a work emerged from obscurity after the last war. A certain amount of intelligent guesswork has therefore been necessary.

I am grateful to all those museums which allowed me access to their catalogue files.

R.C.

1 *Hungarian Landscape 1908*

Inscribed 'OK' b.r.
Oil on canvas, 73.6 × 100.4 cm. ($29 × 39\frac{1}{2}$ in.)
Private Collection, USA
Literature: Hoffmann 1947, no. 8, p. 289; Wingler 1958, no. 8, p. 293, repr. pl. 1

2 *Father Hirsch 1909*

Inscribed 'OK' t.l.
Oil on canvas, 70.5 × 62.5 cm. ($27\frac{3}{4} × 24\frac{5}{8}$ in.)
Neue Galerie der Stadt Linz, Wolfgang-Gurlitt-Museum
Literature: Hoffmann 1947, no. 2, p. 288; Wingler 1958, no. 4, p. 293, repr. in colour pl. 1

3 *The Court Tailor E. Ebenstein 1909*

Inscribed 'OK' b.r.
Oil on canvas, 101.8 × 81.1 cm. (40 × 32 in.)
Art Institute of Chicago, Joseph Winterbotham Collection
Literature: Hoffmann 1947, no. 11, pp. 47, 89, 290; Wingler 1958, no. 10, p. 294 (repr.)

4 *Martha Hirsch 1909*

Inscribed 'OK' b.r.
Oil on canvas, 88 × 70 cm. ($34\frac{5}{8} × 27\frac{1}{2}$ in.)
Private Collection, courtesy Serge Sabarsky Gallery, New York
Literature: Hoffmann 1947, no. 1, pp. 98–9, 288; Wingler 1958, no. 6, p. 293, repr. pl. 12

*5 *Adolf Loos 1909*

Inscribed 'OK' t.r. and '1909' b.r.
Oil on canvas, 74 × 91 cm. ($29\frac{1}{8} × 35\frac{3}{4}$ in.)
Staatliche Museen Preussischer Kulturbesitz, Nationalgalerie, Berlin
Literature: Hoffmann 1947, no. 19, pp. 41–7, 51 n., 95–6, 291–2, repr. pl. X; Wingler 1958, no. 15, p. 294, repr. pl. 5

6 *Felix Albrecht Harta 1909*

Inscribed 'OK' t.r. and '1909' b.r.
Oil on canvas, 73.1 × 52.5 cm. ($28\frac{3}{4} × 20\frac{5}{8}$ in.)
Hirshhorn Museum and Sculpture Garden, Smithsonian Institution, Washington, D.C.
Literature: Hoffmann 1947, no. 20, pp. 98, 292; Wingler 1958, no. 13, p. 294 (repr.)

7 *Peter Altenberg 1909*

Inscribed 'OK/09' b.l.
Oil on canvas, 76 × 71 cm. ($29\frac{7}{8} × 28$ in.)
Private Collection, courtesy Serge Sabarsky Gallery, New York
Literature: Hoffmann 1947, no. 16, pp. 90–4, 291; Wingler 1958, no. 17, p. 295, repr. pl. 11

8 *Dr Emma Veronika Sanders 1909*

Inscribed 'OK' t.r.
Oil on canvas, 82.7 × 56.7 cm. ($32\frac{5}{8} × 22\frac{3}{8}$ in.)
Museum of Modern Art, New York, Gift of Mr and Mrs William Mazer, 1967
Literature: Hoffmann 1947, no. 54, p. 298; Wingler 1958, no. 26, p. 296 (repr.)

9 *Lotte Franzos 1909*

Inscribed 'OK' b.r.
Oil on canvas, 115 × 79.5 cm. ($45\frac{1}{4} × 31\frac{1}{4}$ in.)
Phillips Collection, Washington, D.C.
Literature: Hoffmann 1947, no. 18, pp. 95, 251, repr. pl. VI; Wingler 1958, no. 11, p. 294, repr. pl. 8

10 *Hans Tietze and Erica Tietze-Conrat 1909*

Inscribed 'OK' b.r.
Oil on canvas, 76.5 × 136.2 cm. ($30\frac{1}{8} × 58\frac{5}{8}$ in.)
Museum of Modern Art, New York, Abby Aldrich Rockefeller Fund. 1939
Literature: Hoffmann 1947, no. 15, pp. 99, 290, repr. pl. VII; Wingler 1958, no. 29, p. 296, repr. pl. 25

*11 *Bessie Bruce 1910*

Inscribed 'OK' b.r.
Oil on canvas, 72 × 91 cm. ($28\frac{3}{8} × 35\frac{3}{4}$ in.)
Staatliche Museen Preussischer Kulturbesitz, Nationalgalerie, Berlin
Literature: Hoffmann 1947, no. 24, pp. 96–7, 292–3; Wingler 1958, no. 31, p. 296 (repr.)

12 *Victoria de Montesquiou-Fezensac 1910*

Inscribed 'OK' b.c.
Oil on canvas, 94.6 × 48.9 cm. ($37\frac{1}{4} × 19\frac{1}{4}$ in.)
Cincinnati Art Museum, Bequest of Paul E. Geier
Literature: Hoffmann 1947, no. 38, pp. 100–1, 295, repr. pl. XVIII; Wingler 1958, no. 33, p. 297, repr. pl. 13

13 *Joseph de Montesquiou-Fezensač 1910*

Inscribed 'OK' b.l.
Oil on canvas, 80 × 63 cm. ($31\frac{1}{2} × 24\frac{3}{4}$ in.)
Moderna Museet, Stockholm
Literature: Hoffmann 1947, no. 37, p. 295, repr.
pl. XVII; Wingler 1958, no. 34, p. 297 (repr.)

14 *Conte Verona 1910*

Inscribed 'OK' b.r.
Oil on canvas, 70.6 × 58.7 cm. ($27\frac{3}{4} × 23\frac{1}{8}$ in.)
Kniže Collection
Literature: Hoffmann 1947, no. 39, pp. 97, 295;
Wingler 1958, no. 32, p. 297 (repr.)

15 *Boy with Raised Hand (Hans Reichel)
1910*

Inscribed 'OK' b.r.
Oil on canvas, 69.9 × 65.1 cm. ($27\frac{1}{2} × 25\frac{5}{8}$ in.)
Mr and Mrs Prescott N. Dunbar, New Orleans
Literature: Hoffmann 1947, no. 9, pp. 98, 289,
repr. pl. V; Wingler 1958, no. 20, p. 295, repr.
pl. 6

16 *Herwarth Walden 1910*

Inscribed 'OK' b.r.
Oil on canvas, 100 × 69.3 cm. ($39\frac{3}{8} × 27\frac{1}{4}$ in.)
Staatsgalerie Stuttgart
Literature: Hoffmann 1947, no. 40, pp. 73–6, 84,
295; Wingler 1958, no. 38, p. 297, repr. pl. 21

17 *Paul Scheerbart 1910*

Inscribed 'OK' t.r.
Oil on canvas, 70 × 47 cm. ($27\frac{1}{2} × 18\frac{1}{2}$ in.)
Private Collection, courtesy Serge Sabarsky Gallery,
New York
Literature: Hoffmann 1947, no. 47, pp. 84, 296;
Wingler 1958, no. 41, p. 298, repr. pl. 18

18 *Design for 'Sturm' Poster 1910*

Inscribed 'OK' b.r.
Oil on canvas, 102 × 70 cm. ($40\frac{1}{8} × 27\frac{1}{2}$ in.)
Szépmüvészeti Museum, Budapest

19 *Else Kupfer 1911*

Inscribed 'OK' t.r.
Oil on canvas, 90 × 71.5 cm. ($35\frac{3}{8} × 28\frac{1}{8}$ in.)
Kunsthaus, Zurich
Literature: Hoffmann 1947, no. 36, pp. 99, 101,
294, repr. pl. 15; Wingler 1958, no. 49, p. 299,
repr. pl. 14

20 *Egon Wellesz 1911*

Inscribed 'OK' t.l.
Oil on canvas, 75.5 × 68.9 cm. ($29\frac{3}{4} × 27\frac{1}{8}$ in.)
Hirshhorn Museum and Sculpture Garden,
Smithsonian Institution, Washington, D.C.
Literature: Hoffmann 1947, no. 53, pp. 112, 297;
Wingler 1958, no. 64, p. 300 (repr.)

21 *The Annunciation 1911*

Inscribed 'OK' b.l.
Oil on canvas, 83 × 122.5 cm. ($32\frac{5}{8} × 48\frac{1}{4}$ in.)
Museum am Ostwall, Dortmund
Literature: Hoffmann 1947, no. 52 (as 'The
Visitation'), pp. 101, 297; Wingler 1958, no. 59,
p. 300, repr. pl. 30

22 *Portrait of Mrs Karpeles 1911*

Inscribed 'OK' b.l.
Oil on canvas, 99.6 × 74.2 cm. ($39\frac{1}{4} × 29\frac{1}{4}$ in.)
Hirshhorn Museum and Sculpture Garden,
Smithsonian Institution, Washington, D.C., Gift
of Joseph H. Hirshhorn Foundation, 1966
Literature: Hoffmann 1947, no. 43, pp. 99, 296;
Wingler 1958, no. 65, p. 301 (repr.)

23 *Two Nudes 1912*

Inscribed 'OK' b.l.
Oil on canvas, 146.5 × 82.5 cm. ($57\frac{3}{4} × 32\frac{1}{2}$ in.)
Wellesley College Museum, Gift of Professor and
Mrs John McAndrew
Literature: Hoffmann 1947, no. 70, pp. 113,
299–300; Wingler 1958, no. 76, p. 302 (repr.)

24 *Alma Mahler 1912*

Inscribed 'OK' b.r.
Oil on canvas, 62 × 56 cm. ($24\frac{3}{8} × 22$ in.)
Marlborough Gallery, Inc., New York, and
Marlborough Fine Art (London) Ltd.
Literature: Hoffmann 1947, no. 78 (as 'Portrait of a
Woman'), pp. 116–17, 301; Wingler 1958,
no. 78, p. 302 (repr.)

25 *Self-portrait 1913*

Inscribed 'OK' b.r.
Oil on canvas, 81.6 × 49.5 cm. ($32\frac{1}{8} × 19\frac{1}{2}$ in.)
Museum of Modern Art, New York,
Purchase, 1940
Literature: Hoffmann 1947, no. 80, pp. 114–5,
301, repr. pl. XXI; Wingler 1958, no. 72, p. 301,
(repr.)

26 *Two Nudes (the Lovers) 1913*

Inscribed 'OK' b.c.
Oil on canvas, 163 × 97.5 cm. ($64\frac{1}{4} × 38\frac{3}{8}$ in.)
Museum of Fine Arts, Boston, Bequest of Mrs
Sarah Reed Blodget Platt
Literature: Hoffmann 1947, no. 69, p. 299;
Wingler 1958, no. 77, p. 302 (repr.)

27 *Still-life with Putto and Rabbit 1914*

Inscribed 'OK' b.r.
Oil on canvas, 90 × 120 cm. ($35\frac{1}{2} × 47\frac{1}{4}$ in.)
Marlborough Gallery Inc., New York, and
Marlborough Fine Art (London) Ltd.
Literature: Hoffmann 1947, no. 96 (as 'Still-life
with Cat'), pp. 119, 304; Wingler 1958, no. 95,
p. 304, repr. pl. 40

28 *Franz Hauer 1914*

Inscribed 'OK' t.r.
Oil on canvas, 120 × 106 cm. ($47\frac{1}{4} × 41\frac{3}{4}$ in.)
Museum of Art, Rhode Island School of Design,
Providence, Georgiana Aldrich Fund and
Museum Works of Art, 53.121
Literature: Hoffmann 1947, no. 87, p. 302;
Wingler 1958, no. 92 (as 'Josef Hauer'), p. 304
(repr.)

29 *Emil Löwenbach* 1914

Inscribed 'OK' t.l.
Oil on canvas, 125 × 79 cm. (49¼ × 31⅛ in.)
The Robert Gore Rifkind Foundation,
Beverly Hills, California
Literature: Wingler 1958, no. 100 (as 'E. Ludwig
["The Blind Man"]'), p. 305 repr.

30 *Knight Errant* 1914–15

Inscribed 'OK' b.r.
Oil on canvas, 89.5 × 180.1 cm. (35¼ × 70⅛ in.)
Solomon R. Guggenheim Museum, New York
Literature: Hoffmann 1947, no. 105, pp. 123,
153–4, 305, repr. pl. XXIX; Wingler 1958,
no. 105, p. 305, repr. pl. 44

31 *Heinrich von Neumann* 1916

Not inscribed
Oil on canvas, 90.1 × 59.9 cm. (35½ × 23½ in.)
Harvard University Art Museums (Busch-
Reisinger Museum), Purchase, Museum
Association Fund
Literature: Wingler 1958, no. 106, p. 306, repr.
pl. 38

32 *Lovers with Cat* 1917

Inscribed 'OK' b.l. and '1917' on back of canvas
Oil on canvas, 93.5 × 130.5 cm. (36¾ × 51⅜ in.)
Kunsthaus, Zurich
Literature: Hoffmann 1947, no. 118, pp. 159–60,
308, repr. pl. XXXI; Wingler 1958, no. 116,
p. 307, repr. pl. 46

33 *The Power of Music* 1918–19

Not inscribed
Oil on canvas, 100 × 151.5 cm. (39⅜ × 59⅝ in.)
Stedelijk Van Abbemuseum, Eindhoven
Literature: Hoffmann 1947, no. 119, pp. 160–1,
308; Wingler 1958, no. 130, p. 308, repr. pl. 51

34 *Self-portrait with Doll* 1920–1

Inscribed 'OK' b.l.
Oil on canvas, 80 × 120 cm. (31½ × 47¼ in.)
Staatliche Museen Preussischer Kulturbesitz,
Nationalgalerie, Berlin
Literature: Wingler 1958, no. 144, p. 309, repr.
pl. 56

35 *Dresden, Neustadt II* 1921

Inscribed 'OK' b.l.
Oil on canvas, 59.7 × 80 cm. (23½ × 31½ in.)
Detroit Institute of Arts, City of Detroit purchase
Literature: Hoffmann 1947, no. 125 (as 'Dresden
I'), pp. 165–6, 309; Wingler 1958, no. 135,
p. 309 (repr.)

36 *Gitta Wallerstein* 1921

Inscribed 'OK' t.l.
Oil on canvas, 85 × 60 cm. (33½ × 23⅝ in.)
Private Collection, W. Germany
Literature: Hoffmann 1947, no. 142, p. 311;
Wingler 1958, no. 139, p. 309, repr. pl. 55

37 *Mother and Child (embracing)* 1921

Inscribed 'OK' b.l.
Oil on canvas, 121 × 81 cm. (47⅝ × 37⅞ in.)
Österreichische Galerie, Vienna
Literature: Hoffmann 1947, no. 163, pp. 166–7,
217, 314; Wingler 1958, no. 142, p. 309 (repr.)

38 *Dresden, Neustadt IV* 1921

Inscribed 'OK' b.l.
Oil on canvas, 68.5 × 109.2 cm. (27 × 43 in.)
Private Collection

39 *Girl with Doll* 1921–2

Inscribed 'OK' t.r.
Oil on canvas, 91.5 × 81.2 cm. (36 × 32 in.)
Detroit Institute of Arts, Bequest of Dr Wilhelm
R. Valentiner
Literature: Hoffmann 1947, no. 127, pp. 166,
309–10; Wingler 1958, no. 143, p. 309 (repr.)

40 *The Slave Girl* 1923

Inscribed 'OK' b.l.
Oil on canvas, 110.5 × 80 cm. (43¼ × 31½ in.)
Saint Louis Art Museum, Bequest of Morton D.
May
Literature: Hoffmann 1947, no. 162, p. 314;
Wingler 1958, no. 161, p. 311 (repr.)

41 *Girl with Flowers* 1923

Inscribed 'OK' b.l.
Oil on canvas, 73 × 60 cm. (28¾ × 23⅝ in.)
Marlborough Gallery, Inc., New York, and
Marlborough Fine Art (London) Ltd.
Literature: Wingler 1958, no. 159, p. 311 (repr.)

42 *Lac Léman I* 1923

Not inscribed
Oil on canvas, 80 × 120 cm. (31½ × 47¼ in.)
Private Collection
Literature: Hoffmann 1947, no. 169, pp. 174–5,
315, repr. pl. XXXIV; Wingler 1958, no. 164,
p. 312 (repr.)

43 *Arnold Schoenberg* 1924

Inscribed 'OK' t.l.
Oil on canvas, 96 × 74 cm. (37¾ × 29⅛ in.)
Private Collection, courtesy Serge Sabarsky
Gallery, New York
Literature: Hoffmann 1947, no. 172, pp. 175, 316;
Wingler 1958, no. 171, p. 312, repr. pl. 63

44 *Nancy Cunard* 1924

Inscribed 'OK' b.r.
Oil on canvas, 116 × 73 cm. (45⅝ × 28¾ in.)
Sprengel Museum, Hannover
Literature: Hoffmann 1947, no. 166, pp. 177, 193,
315; Wingler 1958, no. 175, p. 313, repr. pl. 62

45 *Karl Kraus II* 1925

Inscribed and dated on back of canvas
Oil on canvas, 65 × 100 cm. (25⅝ × 39⅜ in.)
Museum Moderner Kunst, Vienna
Literature: Hoffmann 1947, no. 180, pp. 175–6,
317–18, repr. pl. XLI; Wingler 1958, no. 180,
p. 313 (repr.)

46 *The Coast at Dover 1926*

Inscribed 'OK' b.r.
Oil on canvas, 76.5 × 127.5 cm. (30⅛ × 50¼ in.)
Kunstmuseum, Basel
Literature: Hoffmann 1947, no. 202, pp. 178, 321–2; Wingler 1958, no. 212, p. 316, repr. pl. 76

47 *London, large Thames View I 1926*

Inscribed 'OK' b.l.
Oil on canvas, 90 × 130 cm. (35¼ × 51¼ in.)
Albright-Knox Art Gallery, Buffalo, New York, Room of Contemporary Art Fund, 1941
Literature: Hoffmann 1947, no. 205, pp. 186, 322; Wingler 1958, no. 208, p. 316 (repr.)

48 *London, Waterloo Bridge 1926*

Inscribed 'OK' b.r.
Oil on canvas, 89 × 130 cm. (35 × 51 in.)
National Museum of Wales, Cardiff
Literature: Hoffmann 1947, no. 213, pp. 178, 186, 324; Wingler 1958, no. 209, p. 316 (repr.)

49 *Adèle Astaire 1926*

Inscribed 'OK LONDON 26' t.l.
Oil on canvas, 97 × 130.5 cm. (38⅛ × 51⅜ in.)
Kunsthaus, Zurich
Literature: Hoffmann 1947, no. 201, pp. 192–3; Wingler 1958, no. 214, p. 316, repr. pl. 66

50 *Mandrill 1926*

Not inscribed
Oil on canvas, 127.5 × 102.3 cm. (49¾ × 40¼ in.)
Museum Boymans-van Beuningen, Rotterdam
Literature: Hoffmann 1947, no. 207, pp. 178–9, 322–3, repr. pl. XLIII; Wingler 1958, no. 215, p. 316, repr. pl. 82

51 *Deer 1926*

Inscribed 'OK' b.l. and 'OK 1926' on back of canvas
Oil on canvas, 130 × 89 cm. (51⅛ × 35 in.)
Private Collection, W. Germany
Literature: Hoffmann 1947, no. 209 (as 'Roes'), pp. 179, 192, 323; Wingler 1958, no. 217, p. 316, repr. pl. 83

52 *Elza Temary 1926–7*

Not inscribed
Oil on canvas, 93 × 132 cm. (36⅝ × 52 in.)
Private Collection
Literature: Hoffmann 1947, no. 215, pp. 192–3, 324; Wingler 1958, no. 222, p. 317, repr. pl. 38

53 *Fritz Wolff-Kniže 1927*

Inscribed 'OK 27' b.l.
Oil on canvas, 110 × 88 cm. (43¼ × 34½ in.)
Kniže Collection
Literature: Hoffmann 1947, no. 221, p. 326; Wingler 1958, no. 225, p. 317 (repr.)

54 *Lyons 1927*

Inscribed 'OK' b.l.
Oil on canvas, 97.1 × 130.2 cm. (38¼ × 51¼ in.)
Phillips Collection, Washington, D.C.
Literature: Hoffmann 1947, no. 218, pp. 179, 181, 187, 325, repr. pl. XLIX; Wingler 1958, no. 232, p. 318, repr. in colour pl. XVI

55 *The Marabout of Temacine (Sidi Ahmet Ben Tidjani) 1928*

Inscribed 'OK' t.l.
Oil on canvas, 98.5 × 130.5 cm. (38¾ × 51⅜ in.)
Private Collection
Literature: Hoffmann 1947, no. 226, pp. 180–1, 193–4, 327, repr. pl. LII; Wingler 1958, no. 237, p. 318, repr. pl. 88

56 *Marczell von Nemeš 1928*

Not inscribed
Oil on canvas, 135 × 96 cm. (53⅛ × 37¾ in.)
Neue Galerie der Stadt Linz, Wolfgang-Gurlitt-Museum
Literature: Hoffmann 1947, no. 234, p. 238, repr. pl. LXI; Wingler 1958, no. 245, p. 319, repr. in colour pl. XVIII

57 *Arab Women and Child 1929*

Inscribed 'OK' b.r.
Oil on canvas, 88.5 × 128 cm. (34¾ × 50⅜ in.)
Private Collection (on loan to the Tate Gallery)
Literature: Wingler 1958, no. 246, p. 319 (repr.)

58 *Pan (Trudl with Goat) 1931*

Inscribed 'OK' b.r.
Oil on canvas, 87 × 130 cm. (34¼ × 51⅛ in.)
Sprengel Museum, Hannover
Literature: Hoffmann 1947, no. 244, pp. 216–17, 330; Wingler 1958, no. 258, p. 321 (repr.)

59 *Vienna, View from the Wilhelminenberg 1931*

Inscribed 'O Kokoschka/31' b.l.
Oil on canvas, 92 × 134 cm. (36¼ × 52¾ in.)
Historisches Museum, Vienna
Literature: Hoffmann 1947, no. 248, pp. 196–7, 330; Wingler 1958, no. 260, p. 321, repr. in colour, pl. XIX

★60 *Self-portrait with Cap 1932*

Inscribed 'OK' b.r.
Oil on canvas, 98 × 71 cm. (38⅝ × 28 in.)
Private Collection, Epsom
Literature: Hoffmann 1947, no. 254, pp. 194–5, 331; Wingler 1958, no. 263, p. 322, repr. in colour pl. XXI

61 *Mother and Child (Trudl with Noh Mask) 1934*

Inscribed 'OK' b.r.
Oil on canvas, 56 × 75 cm. (22 × 29½ in.)
Galerie Würthle, Vienna
Literature: Hoffmann 1947, no. 261, pp. 217, 332; Wingler 1958, no. 281, p. 323, repr. pl. 95

62 *Prague, View from the Villa Kramář 1934–5*

Inscribed 'OK' b.l.
Oil on canvas, 90 × 121 cm. (35½ × 47⅜ in.)
Národní Galerie, Prague
Literature: Hoffmann 1947, no. 273, pp. 218–19, 333; Wingler 1958, no. 290, p. 324, repr. pl. 99

63 *Thomas G. Masaryk 1935–6*

Inscribed 'OK' b.l.
Oil on canvas, 97.7 × 131 cm. (38½ × 51½ in.)
Museum of Art, Carnegie Institute, Pittsburgh,
Pennsylvania, Patrons Art Fund 1956
Literature: Hoffmann 1947, no. 263, pp. 210–14,
332, repr. pl. LXVII; Wingler 1958, no. 298,
p. 325, repr. pl. 97

64 *Olda Palkovská 1935–7*

Not inscribed
Oil on canvas, 90 × 67 cm. (35½ × 26⅜ in.)
Private Collection

65 *Prague, Nostalgia 1938*

Inscribed 'OK' b.l.
Oil on canvas, 56 × 76 cm. (22 × 30 in.)
Lord Croft
Literature: Hoffmann 1947, no. 285, pp. 230–1,
335; Wingler 1958, no. 314, p. 328 (repr.)

66 *Michael Croft 1938–9*

Inscribed 'OK' b.r. and
'1939   NOBODY COULD
IN DIRTY   PA[I]NT THIS
EXILE,   WORK, BUT
ILL AND   NOBODY
POOR   COULD VALUE
           IT TOO, AT

THIS DIRTY TIME,
WHEN THEY ALL, EVERY
WHERE, ARE HUNTING
THE ARTIST AND BECOME
SLAVES THEMSELVES' on back of canvas
Oil on canvas, 76.2 × 63.7 cm. (30 × 25⅛ in.)
Lord Croft
Literature: Hoffmann 1947, no. 291, pp. 225, 335,
repr. pl. LXXVI; Wingler 1958, no. 315, p. 328
(repr.)

67 *Posy Croft 1939*

Not inscribed
Oil on canvas, 76.2 × 63.5 cm. (30 × 25 in.)
Private Collection
Literature: Hoffmann 1947, no. 292, pp. 225, 336;
Wingler 1958, no. 316, p. 328 (repr.)

68 *Summer II (Zrání) 1938–40*

Inscribed 'Zrání/OK' b.l.
Oil on canvas, 68.3 × 82.9 cm. (26⅞ × 35⅛ in.)
Scottish National Gallery of Modern Art,
Edinburgh
Literature: Hoffmann 1947, no. 284, pp. 220, 226,
230, 334, repr. pl. LXXI; Wingler 1958,
no. 321, p. 328, repr. pl. 101

69 *The Red Egg 1940–1*

Inscribed 'OK' b.r. and 'a red Egg for/Manchester
– Christianity wishes kindly/OK, London, 1939,
Easter time' on back of canvas
Oil on canvas, 63 × 76 cm. (25 × 30 in.)
Národní Galerie, Prague
Literature: Hoffmann 1947, no. 293, pp. 234–5,
336, repr. pl. LXXVII; Wingler 1958, no. 322,
p. 328, repr. pl. 106

70 *Anschluss – Alice in Wonderland 1942*

Inscribed 'OK' b.r. and 'THE "ansluss" by
OK/1939' diagonally across back of canvas
Oil on canvas, 63.5 × 73.6 cm. (25 × 30 in.)
Wiener Städtische Wechselseitige
Versicherungsanstalt
Literature: Hoffmann 1947, no. 295, pp. 235, 238,
336, repr. pl. LXXVIII; Wingler 1958, no. 323,
p. 328 (repr.)

71 *Loreley 1941–2*

Inscribed 'OK' b.r. and 'LORELEY – by
O.K./1942' on back of canvas
Oil on canvas, 63.5 × 76.4 cm. (25 × 30 in.)
Private Collection (on loan to the Tate Gallery)
Literature: Hoffmann 1947, no. 296, pp. 236, 336,
repr. pl. LXXIX; Wingler 1958, no. 325,
p. 329, repr. pl. 107

72 *Marianne Maquis 1942*

Inscribed 'OK' b.l. and 'MAquis by O.K./1942'
diagonally across back of canvas and 'Second
Front' in pencil on stretcher
Oil on canvas, 63.5 × 76 cm. (25 × 30 in.)
Private Collection (on loan to the Tate Gallery)
Literature: Hoffmann 1947, no. 297, p. 336, repr.
pl. LXXX; Wingler 1958, no. 326, p. 329 (repr.)

73 *Ivan Maisky 1942–3*

Inscribed 'OK' b.r. and 'Mr. MAISKY /
London 1942 / for Red Cross unit Stalingrad /
spend by OK' on back of canvas
Oil on canvas, 102 × 77 cm. (40⅛ × 30¼ in.)
Tate Gallery, London
Literature: Hoffmann 1947, no. 300, pp. 238–9,
336 repr. in colour pl. 4; Wingler 1958, no. 328,
p. 329, repr. pl. 105

74 *What we are fighting for 1943*

Inscribed 'OK / london 43' b.l.
Oil on canvas, 116.5 × 152 cm. (45⅞ × 59¹³⁄₁₆ in.)
Kunsthaus, Zurich
Literature: Hoffmann 1947, no. 301, pp. 236–8,
337, repr. pl. LXXXI; Wingler 1958, no. 329,
p. 329 (repr.)

75 *Ullapool 1945*

Inscribed 'OK' b.l.
Oil on canvas, 61.5 × 91.5 cm. (24¼ × 26 in.)
Basil Trakman
Literature: Wingler 1958, no. 335, p. 330 (repr.)

76 *Kathleen, Countess of Drogheda 1944–6*

Inscribed 'OK' b.l.
Oil on canvas, 102 × 76 cm. (40⅛ × 30 in.)
Private Collection
Literature: Hoffmann 1947, no. 307, p. 337, repr.
in an earlier state pl. LXXXII; Wingler 1958,
no. 336, p. 330, repr. pl. 109

77 *Acrobat's Family 1946*

Inscribed 'OK' b.r.
Oil on canvas, 50 × 61 cm. (19¾ × 24 in.)
Private Collection, W. Germany
Literature: Wingler 1958, no. 337 (as 'Slum'),
p. 330 (repr.)

78 *Matterhorn I 1947*

Inscribed 'OK' b.l.
Oil on canvas, 76.2 × 100.4 cm. (30 × 39½ in.)
Private Collection
Literature: Wingler 1958, no. 343, p. 330 (repr.)

79 *Werner Reinhart 1947*

Inscribed 'OK' on back of canvas
Oil on canvas, 80 × 120 cm. ($31\frac{1}{2} \times 47\frac{1}{4}$ in.)
Kunstmuseum, Winterthur
Literature: Wingler 1958, no. 346, p. 331, repr. pl. 112

80 *Venice, Santa Maria della Salute III 1948*

Inscribed 'OK' b.l.
Oil on canvas, 85 × 110 cm. ($33\frac{1}{2} \times 43\frac{1}{2}$ in.)
Italian Family Collection
Literature: Wingler 1958, no. 351, p. 331 (repr.)

81 *Self-portrait (Fiesole) 1948*

Inscribed 'OK' t.l.
Oil on canvas, 65.5 × 55 cm. ($25\frac{3}{4} \times 21\frac{5}{8}$ in.)
Private Collection
Literature: Wingler 1958, no. 353, p. 331 (repr.)

82 *Cardinal dalla Costa 1948*

Not inscribed
Oil on canvas, 97.5 × 71.5 cm. ($38\frac{3}{4} \times 28\frac{1}{8}$ in.)
Phillips Collection, Washington, D.C.
Literature: Wingler 1958, no. 355, p. 332, repr. pl. 108

83 *The Feilchenfeldt Brothers 1952*

Inscribed 'OK' b.r.
Oil on canvas, 90 × 135 cm. ($35\frac{3}{8} \times 53\frac{1}{8}$ in.)
Mrs W. Feilchenfeldt, Zurich
Literature: Wingler 1958, no. 375, p. 334 (repr.)

84 *Herodotus 1960–4*

Not inscribed
Oil on canvas, 180 × 120 cm. ($70\frac{7}{8} \times 47\frac{1}{4}$ in.)
Österreichische Galerie, Vienna

85 *The Rejected Lover 1966*

Inscribed 'OK' b.r.
Oil on canvas, 81 × 117 cm. (32 × 46 in.)
Private Collection

86 *New York, Manhattan with the Empire State Building 1966*

Inscribed 'OK' b.l.
Oil on canvas, 101.5 × 137 cm. (40 × 54 in.)
Private Collection

87 *Morning and Evening (The Power of Music II) 1966*

Inscribed 'OK' b.l.
Oil on canvas, 100 × 130 cm. ($39\frac{3}{8} \times 51\frac{1}{8}$ in.)
Private Collection

88 *Self-portrait 1969*

Inscribed 'OK' t.l.
Oil on canvas, 90.5 × 70.4 cm. ($35\frac{5}{8} \times 27\frac{3}{4}$ in.)
Private Collection (on loan to the Tate Gallery)

89 *Agatha Christie 1969*

Inscribed 'OK' t.r.
Oil on canvas, 81 × 112 cm. ($31\frac{7}{8} \times 44$ in.)
Private Collection

90 *The Duke and Duchess of Hamilton 1969*

Inscribed 'OK' b.l.
Oil on canvas, 89.8 × 129.8 cm. ($35\frac{3}{8} \times 51\frac{1}{8}$ in.)
The Duke of Hamilton (on loan to the Scottish National Portrait Gallery)

91 *Time, Gentlemen Please 1971–2*

Inscribed 'OK' b.l. and 'TIME, gentlemen/please.' t.l.
Oil on canvas, 130 × 100 cm. ($51\frac{1}{4} \times 39\frac{3}{8}$ in.)
Private Collection

92 *Peer Gynt 1973*

Inscribed 'OK' b.r.
Oil on canvas, 115 × 89 cm. ($45\frac{1}{4} \times 35$ in.)
Private Collection

93 *Theseus and Antiope 1958/74*

Not inscribed
Oil on canvas, 195 × 165 cm. ($76\frac{3}{4} \times 65$ in.)
Private Collection

94 *Standing Nude Boy* c.*1906*

Inscribed 'OK' b.r.
Pencil and watercolour, 44.9 × 31.5 cm. ($17\frac{5}{8} \times 12\frac{3}{8}$ in.)
Private Collection, W. Germany

95 *Study for* The Dreaming Youths *1907*

Inscribed 'OK' b.r. and 'Studie zu den / "Traumenden Knaben" / Wien 1907 OK' b.l.
Pencil, 37 × 28.6 cm. ($14\frac{1}{2} \times 11\frac{1}{4}$ in.)
Kunstmuseum, Basel, Kupferstichkabinett

96 *Three Studies of Nude Girl* c.*1907*

Inscribed 'OK' b.r.
Pencil, 45 × 31.9 cm. ($17\frac{3}{4} \times 12\frac{1}{2}$ in.)
Národní Galerie, Prague

97 *The Acrobat's Daughter* c.*1907*

Inscribed 'OKokoschka' b.l.
Pencil, 43.2 × 29.2 cm. ($17 \times 11\frac{1}{2}$ in.)
Private Collection, London

98 *The Acrobat* c.*1907*

Inscribed (later) with authentication '1907' and 'OKokoschka' b.l.
Pencil, 44.5 × 30.5 cm. ($17\frac{1}{2} \times 12$ in.)
Private Collection, London

99 *Nude with Back Turned* c.*1907*

Inscribed 'OK' c.
Watercolour, crayon, pencil and ink, 45.1 × 31.1 cm. ($17\frac{3}{4} \times 12\frac{1}{4}$ in.)
Museum of Modern Art, New York, Rose Gershwin Fund

100 *Standing Nude Girl* c.*1907–8*

Inscribed 'OK' b.r.
Pencil, watercolour and ink, 44.8 × 30.2 cm.
($17\frac{5}{8} × 11\frac{3}{4}$ in.)
Private Collection, W. Germany

101 *Two Girls (trying on clothes)* c.*1907–8*

Inscribed 'OK' b.l.
Pencil, watercolour and gouache, 44 × 30.8 cm.
($17\frac{1}{4} × 12\frac{1}{8}$ in.)
Private Collection, W. Germany

102 *Japanese Fisherman 1908*

Inscribed 'OK' c.r.
Gouache, pen and ink over pencil,
20.8 × 16.5 cm. ($8\frac{1}{8} × 6\frac{1}{2}$ in.)
Museum am Ostwall, Dortmund

103 *Storm at Sea 1908*

Inscribed 'OK' b.l.
Gouache, pen and ink over pencil,
20.9 × 16.7 cm. ($8\frac{1}{4} × 6\frac{1}{2}$ in.)
Kunstmuseum, Basel, Kupferstichkabinett

104 *Murder of a Woman*, Illustration to
    Murderer Hope of Women *1908–9*

Inscribed 'OK' b.r.
Pencil, ink and watercolour, 30.8 × 25.8 cm.
($12\frac{1}{8} × 10\frac{1}{8}$ in.)
Los Angeles County Museum of Art, The Robert
Gore Rifkind Center for German Expressionist
Studies, M.82.287.85

105 *Illustration to* Murderer Hope of
    Women *1910*

Inscribed 'OK' c.l. (on arm)
Pen and ink, 24.5 × 18.2 cm. ($9\frac{5}{8} × 7\frac{1}{4}$ in.)
Graphische Sammlung, Staatsgalerie Stuttgart

106 *Self-portrait ('Sturm' Poster) 1910*

Inscribed in stone 'OK' b.r.
Colour lithograph, 67.3 × 44.7 cm.
($26\frac{1}{2} × 17\frac{5}{8}$ in.)
The Robert Gore Rifkind Foundation,
Beverly Hills, California

107 *Karl Kraus I 1910*

Inscribed 'OK' c.r.
Ink, 29.5 × 20.5 cm. ($11\frac{5}{8} × 8\frac{1}{8}$ in.)
Walter Feilchenfeldt, Zurich

108 *Herwarth Walden 1910*

Inscribed 'OK' b.c.
Pen and ink over pencil, 28.7 × 22.2 cm.
($11\frac{1}{4} × 8\frac{3}{4}$ in.)
Harvard University Art Museums (Fogg Art
Museum), Purchase, Friends of Art and Music at
Harvard

109 *Paul Scheerbart 1910*

Inscribed 'OK' b.r.
Pen and ink over pencil, 31.6 × 20.8 cm.
($12\frac{1}{2} × 8\frac{1}{8}$ in.)
Graphische Sammlung, Staatsgalerie Stuttgart

110 *Lotte Franzos* c.*1911*

Inscribed 'OK' b.r.
Black crayon, 44.8 × 31.6 cm. ($17\frac{5}{8} × 12\frac{3}{8}$ in.)
Museum Folkwang, Essen

111 *Dr Fanina W. Halle* c.*1911*

Inscribed 'OK' b.r.
Black pastel, 45 × 30.5 cm. ($17\frac{3}{4} × 12$ in.)
Tate Gallery, London

112 *Standing Nude* c.*1911*

Inscribed 'OK' b.l.
Black crayon and charcoal, 45.5 × 31.5 cm.
($17\frac{7}{8} × 12\frac{3}{8}$ in.)
Private Collection

113 *Standing Nude* c.*1911*

Inscribed 'OK' b.l.
Black crayon and charcoal, 45.5 × 31.5 cm.
($17\frac{7}{8} × 12\frac{3}{8}$ in.)
Private Collection

114 *Reclining Nude* c.*1911*

Inscribed 'OK' b.l.
Charcoal, 31.5 × 45 cm. ($12\frac{3}{8} × 17\frac{3}{4}$ in.)
Private Collection

115 *Sleeping Nude* c.*1911*

Inscribed 'OK' c.l.
Black crayon and watercolour, 31.5 × 45.5 cm.
($12\frac{3}{8} × 17\frac{7}{8}$ in.)
Private Collection, W. Germany

116 *Seated Nude with Raised Arm* c.*1911*

Inscribed 'OK' c.r. and 'O Kokoschka 1910' b.r.
Black crayon and watercolour, 44.5 × 29.8 cm.
($17\frac{1}{2} × 11\frac{3}{4}$ in.)
Private Collection, W. Germany

117 *Seated Woman* c.*1911–12*

Inscribed 'OK' b.r. and 'O Kokoschka 1911' b.l.
Black crayon and watercolour, 31.2 × 45 cm.
($12\frac{1}{4} × 17\frac{3}{4}$ in.)
Private Collection, W. Germany

118 *Reclining Woman Leaning on Elbow*
    c.*1911–12*

Inscribed 'OK' b.r.
Black crayon and watercolour, 30.8 × 43 cm.
($12\frac{1}{8} × 17$ in.)
Galerie Würthle, Vienna

119 *Reclining Woman* c.*1911–12*

Inscribed 'OK' b.c.
Black crayon and watercolour, 29.5 × 35.3 cm.
($11\frac{5}{8} × 13\frac{7}{8}$ in.)
Solomon R. Guggenheim Museum, New York

120 *The Savoyard Boy (half-length) c.1912*

Inscribed 'OK' b.r.
Black crayon, 39×30.3 cm. ($15\frac{3}{8} \times 12$ in.)
Art Institute of Chicago, Gift of Mrs William O.
Hunt 1967.48

121 *The Savoyard Boy (reclining) c.1912*

Inscribed 'OK' b.r.
Black crayon and watercolour, 45.1×31.7 cm.
($17\frac{3}{4} \times 12\frac{1}{2}$ in.)
Graphische Sammlung, Staatsgalerie, Stuttgart

122 *Alma Mahler 1912*

Inscribed 'Am 12. April 1912 OK' b.r.
Black crayon, 44.5×30.7 cm. ($17\frac{1}{2} \times 12\frac{1}{8}$ in.)
Museum Folkwang, Essen

123 *Karl Kraus II 1912*

Inscribed 'OK' c.r. and 'Karl Kraus / 15 Juli
1912 Wien' b.
Black crayon and charcoal, 44×28 cm.
($17\frac{1}{4} \times 11$ in.)
Private Collection

124 *Wilhelm Köhler 1912*

Inscribed 'OK' b.r.
Black crayon and ink, 42×31.7 cm.
($16\frac{1}{2} \times 12\frac{1}{2}$ in.)
Willard B. Golovin, New York

125 *Alma Mahler 1913*

Inscribed '17.VI.13 OK' b.l.
Black crayon, 49.7×34 cm. ($19\frac{5}{8} \times 13\frac{3}{8}$ in.)
Art Institute of Chicago, Anonymous Gift in
honor of Dr John Gedo

126 *Crouching Nude 1913*

Inscribed 'OK' b.l.
Ink and watercolour, 45×30.8 cm.
($17\frac{3}{4} \times 12\frac{1}{8}$ in.)
Marlborough Gallery, Inc., New York, and
Marlborough Fine Art (London) Ltd.

127 *Young Woman Reclining on Her Elbow
1913*

Inscribed 'OK' b.c.
Black chalk and watercolour, 32.2×44.5 cm.
($12\frac{5}{8} \times 17\frac{1}{2}$ in.)
Marlborough Gallery, Inc., New York, and
Marlborough Fine Art (London) Ltd.

128 *The Meeting 1913*

Not inscribed
Black crayon and watercolour, 42×30 cm.
($16\frac{1}{2} \times 11\frac{3}{4}$ in.)
Private Collection

129 *Tre Croci 1913*

Inscribed 'OK 1913' b.l.
Black crayon, 26×34.5 cm. ($10\frac{1}{4} \times 13\frac{5}{8}$ in.)
Private Collection, W. Germany

130 *Study for* Bach Cantata *1914*

Inscribed 'OK' c.l.
Black crayon and charcoal, 48.2×31.5 cm.
($19 \times 12\frac{3}{8}$ in.)
Private Collection, W. Germany

131 *Study for* Bach Cantata *1914*

Inscribed 'OK' b.l.
Pencil and black crayon, 49.5×35.2 cm.
($19\frac{1}{2} \times 13\frac{7}{8}$ in.)
Private Collection, W. Germany

132 *Portrait of a Lady 1916*

Inscribed 'OK / 11.V.16' b.r.
Black crayon, 56.5×41.5 cm. ($22\frac{1}{4} \times 16\frac{3}{8}$ in.)
Harvard University Art Museums (Fogg Art
Museum), Gift of James N. Rosenberg in honor of
Paul J. Sachs

133 *Portrait of a Lady 1916*

Inscribed 'OK / 1916' b.r.
Black crayon, 68×47 cm. ($26\frac{3}{4} \times 18\frac{1}{2}$ in.)
Art Institute of Chicago, Gift of Margaret Blake
1946.430

134 *Adolf Loos 1916*

Inscribed 'OK 13.II.1916' b.r.
Pencil and watercolour, 64×48.6 cm.
($25\frac{1}{8} \times 19\frac{1}{8}$ in.)
Kunsthaus, Zurich

135 *Rudolf Blümner 1916*

Inscribed 'OK' b.r.
Brush and ink, 35×30.5 cm. ($13\frac{3}{4} \times 12$ in.)
Private Collection, W. Germany

136 *Hugo Erfurth 1916*

Inscribed 'OK' b.r. and '1916' b.l.
Black crayon, 48×35 cm. ($18\frac{7}{8} \times 13\frac{3}{4}$ in.)
Private Collection, W. Germany

137 *Crucifixion 1917*

Inscribed 'OK' b.r.
Blue crayon, 39.3×30 cm. ($15\frac{1}{2} \times 11\frac{3}{4}$ in.)
Private Collection, W. Germany

138 *Standing Girl c.1919*

Inscribed 'O Kokoschka' b.r.
Ink, 68.5×48 cm. (27×19 in.)
Marlborough Gallery, Inc., New York, and
Marlborough Fine Art (London) Ltd.

139 *Portrait of a Woman c.1920–22*

Inscribed 'O Kokoschka' b.r. with dedication to
Carl Moll t.r.
Black crayon, 70.5×50 cm. ($27\frac{3}{4} \times 19\frac{5}{8}$ in.)
Private Collection, courtesy Galerie St Etienne,
New York

140 *Portrait of Ruth Landshoff 1920*

Inscribed 'OK' b.l.
Black chalk, 69.5×48 cm. ($27\frac{3}{8} \times 18\frac{7}{8}$ in.)
Marlborough Gallery, Inc., New York, and
Marlborough Fine Art (London) Ltd.

141 *Study for* The Concert *1920*

Inscribed 'O Kokoschka / 1920 / zum "Concert"' t.l.
Black crayon, 67.7 × 49.8 cm. (26$\frac{5}{8}$ × 19$\frac{5}{8}$ in.)
Private Collection, W. Germany

142 *Self-portrait 1920*

Inscribed '1920' and 'Oskar' with dedication to Bohuslav Kokoschka t.r.
Black crayon, 68 × 47 cm. (26$\frac{3}{4}$ × 18$\frac{1}{2}$ in.)
Galerie Pels-Leusden, W. Berlin

143 *Hugo Erfurth 1921*

Inscribed 'O Kokoschka 15.IV.21' b.r.
Ink, 70.2 × 52 cm. (27$\frac{5}{8}$ × 20$\frac{1}{2}$ in.)
Private Collection

144 *Hugo Erfurth 1921*

Inscribed 'OK' b.r.
Ink, 69.5 × 52 cm. (27$\frac{3}{8}$ × 20$\frac{1}{2}$ in.)
Museum Folkwang, Essen

145 *Bending Girl* c.*1921*

Inscribed 'O Kokoschka' b.r.
Brush and ink, 39.3 × 30 cm. (15$\frac{1}{2}$ × 11$\frac{3}{4}$ in.)
Private Collection, W. Germany

146 *Girl Resting on Elbows* c.*1921*

Inscribed 'O Kokoschka' b.r.
Brush and ink, 46.5 × 63.2 cm. (18$\frac{1}{4}$ × 24$\frac{7}{8}$ in.)
Kunsthaus, Zurich

147 *Seated Girl 1921*

Inscribed 'O Kokoschka / Dresden, 1921' b.l.
Ink and watercolour, 52 × 71 cm. (20$\frac{1}{2}$ × 28 in.)
Private Collection, W. Germany

148 *Seated Woman 1921*

Inscribed 'O Kokoschka / 2. Dez. 21' t.r.
Watercolour, 70.5 × 51.7 cm. (27$\frac{3}{4}$ × 20$\frac{3}{8}$ in.)
Museum of Modern Art, New York, Gift of Myrtil Frank

149 *Fatne Khalil* c.*1921*

Inscribed 'O Kokoschka' b.c. and 'Fatne Khalil' b.r.
Watercolour, 69.2 × 50.8 cm. (27$\frac{1}{4}$ × 20 in.)
Marlborough Gallery, Inc., New York, and Marlborough Fine Art (London) Ltd.

150 *Portrait of a Lady* c.*1921*

Inscribed 'O Kokoschka' t.l.
Black crayon, 70.1 × 49.6 cm. (27$\frac{5}{8}$ × 19$\frac{1}{2}$ in.)
Private Collection, W. Germany

151 *Portrait of a Child* c.*1921*

Inscribed 'O Kokoschka' t.r.
Black crayon and coloured wax crayon, 70 × 50 cm. (27$\frac{1}{2}$ × 19$\frac{3}{4}$ in.)
Private Collection, W. Germany

152 *Reclining Nude* c.*1923*

Inscribed 'O Kokoschka' b.r.
Watercolour, 50.7 × 69.5 cm. (20 × 27$\frac{1}{2}$ in.)
Willard B. Golovin, New York

153 *Oriental Girl with Jug 1923*

Inscribed 'O Kokoschka' b.r. and 'Dresden 24.1.23' with dedication to Walter Feilchenfeldt t.l.
Watercolour, 71 × 52 cm. (28 × 20$\frac{1}{2}$ in.)
Private Collection, Zurich

154 *Circus* c.*1927*

Inscribed 'OK' and 'zu "Circus" / Für Victor D' b.r.
Black crayon, 70 × 50 cm. (27$\frac{1}{2}$ × 19$\frac{3}{4}$ in.)
Galerie Würthle, Vienna

155 *Trudl 1931*

Inscribed 'O Kokoschka' b.l.
Black crayon, 35.2 × 49.8 cm. (13$\frac{7}{8}$ × 19$\frac{5}{8}$ in.)
Private Collection, W. Germany

156 *Trudl with Arms Stretching Forward 1931*

Inscribed 'O Kokoschka' b.r.
Black crayon, 49.6 × 35.6 cm. (19$\frac{1}{2}$ × 14 in.)
Private Collection, W. Germany

157 *Study for 'Thomas G. Masaryk' 1935*

Inscribed 'O Kokoschka' c.r.
Black crayon, 68 × 47 cm. (26$\frac{3}{4}$ × 18$\frac{1}{2}$ in.)
Private Collection

158 *Olda 1935*

Not inscribed
Blue crayon, 45 × 35.5 cm. (17$\frac{3}{4}$ × 14 in.)
Private Collection

159 *F. Garcia Lorca 1936*

Inscribed 'OK' b.r. and 'der ermordete spanische Volksdichter / Frederico Garcia Lorca' c.
Pen and ink, 28.5 × 18 cm. (11$\frac{1}{4}$ × 7$\frac{1}{8}$ in.)
Národní Galerie, Prague

160 *Self-portrait 1936*

Inscribed 'O Kokoschka / 1 4 36' b.r.
Blue crayon, 43.8 × 34.6 cm. (17$\frac{1}{4}$ × 13$\frac{5}{8}$ in.)
Saint Louis Art Museum, Gift of Mr and Mrs Morton D. May 577:1957

161 *Olda with Crown of Flowers 1938*

Inscribed 'O Kokoschka / Prag 38' b.r.
Brown crayon, 43.5 × 35 cm. (17$\frac{1}{8}$ × 13$\frac{3}{4}$ in.)
Private Collection

162 *Polperro I 1939*

Inscribed 'Polperro / O Kokoschka 39' b.r.
Watercolour and pencil, 38 × 54.5 cm. (15 × 21$\frac{1}{2}$ in.)
Lord Croft

163 *Polperro II 1939*

Inscribed 'Polperro / O Kokoschka 39' b.l.
Watercolour and pencil, 37.5 × 55.2 cm.
($14\frac{3}{4} \times 21\frac{3}{4}$ in.)
Lord Croft

164 *Polperro III 1939*

Inscribed 'O Kokoschka / Polperro 39' b.l.
Watercolour and pencil, 31 × 45.2 cm.
($12\frac{1}{8} \times 17\frac{7}{8}$ in.)
Lord Croft

165 *Polperro IV 1939*

Inscribed 'Polperro / O Kokoschka 39' b.r.
Watercolour and pencil, 36 × 43.5 cm.
($12\frac{1}{8} \times 17\frac{1}{8}$ in.)
Lord Croft

166 *Polperro V 1939*

Inscribed 'Polperro / O Kokoschka 39' b.r.
Watercolour and pencil, 36.5 × 53.3 cm.
($14\frac{3}{8} \times 21$ in.)
Lord Croft

167 *Polperro VI 1939*

Not inscribed
Watercolour and pencil, 37.5 × 53.3 cm
($14\frac{3}{4} \times 21$ in.)
Lord Croft

168 *Summer Flowers, Elrig 1941*

Inscribed 'O Kokoschka 41' b.r.
Watercolour, 63.2 × 46.6 cm. ($25\frac{7}{8} \times 24\frac{3}{4}$ in.)
Private Collection

169 *Mushrooms 1942*

Inscribed 'O Kokoschka 1942' b.c.
Watercolour, 48 × 63 cm. ($18\frac{7}{8} \times 24\frac{3}{4}$ in.)
Private Collection

170 *Fish 1942*

Inscribed 'O Kokoschka 42' b.l.
Watercolour, 47.8 × 62.5 cm. ($18\frac{3}{4} \times 24\frac{5}{8}$ in.)
Private Collection

171 *Study for 'Ivan Maisky' 1942*

Not inscribed
Coloured pencil, 35.5 × 25.3 cm. (14×10 in.)
Tate Gallery, London

172 *Study for 'Ivan Maisky' 1942*

Not inscribed
Coloured pencil, 35.5 × 25.3 cm. (14×10 in.)
Tate Gallery, London

173 *Study for 'Scottish Coast' 1941*

Inscribed with dedication 'Neujahr 1942' and
'Olda & OK' on back of card
Coloured pencil, 5 × 9 cm. ($2 \times 3\frac{1}{2}$ in.)
Private Collection, W. Germany

174 *Duck Shoot 1943*

Inscribed 'O Kokoschka 1943' b.r.
Watercolour, 63.2 × 48.2 cm. ($24\frac{7}{8} \times 19$ in.)
Private Collection

175 *Dead Pheasant 1944*

Inscribed 'O Kokoschka 1944' b.l.
Watercolour, 48 × 63 cm. ($18\frac{7}{8} \times 24\frac{3}{4}$ in.)
Private Collection

176 *Study for 'Kathleen, Countess of
    Drogheda' 1944*

Not inscribed
Coloured pencil, pastel and crayon, 100 × 80 cm.
($39\frac{3}{8} \times 31\frac{1}{2}$ in.)
Musée Jenisch, Vevey

177 *Doris with Cat I 1945*

Inscribed 'O Kokoschka 1945' b.r.
Watercolour, 63.5 × 50 cm. ($25 \times 19\frac{5}{8}$ in.)
Private Collection

178 *Doris with Cat II 1945*

Inscribed 'O Kokoschka 1945' b.c.
Watercolour, 63.5 × 50.5 cm. ($25 \times 19\frac{7}{8}$ in.)
Private Collection

179 *Lobster 1946*

Inscribed with dedication to Alfred Marnau
'O Kokoschka / London, 46' b.l.
Watercolour, 53.2 × 68.6 cm. (21×27 in.)
Estate of Senta and Alfred Marnau

180 *Study for 'Matterhorn I' 1947*

Not inscribed
Coloured pencil, 29.2 × 42 cm. ($11\frac{1}{2} \times 16\frac{1}{2}$ in.)
Private Collection, W. Germany

181 *Mary Magdalene 1953*

Inscribed 'OK 53' b.r.
Coloured pencil, 38 × 28 cm. (15×11 in.)
Estate of Senta and Alfred Marnau

182 *Michael Tippett 1963*

Inscribed 'O Kokoschka / 63' b.l.
Black crayon, 62.2 × 48.2 cm. ($24\frac{1}{2} \times 19$ in.)
Private Collection

183 *Self-portrait 1964*

Inscribed 'O Kokoschka / 64' b.r.
Watercolour, 61.5 × 49 cm. ($24\frac{1}{4} \times 19\frac{1}{4}$ in.)
Private Collection, W. Germany

184 *Irises 1972*

Inscribed 'O Kokoschka / V.72' b.l.
Watercolour, 65 × 50.3 cm. ($25\frac{1}{2} \times 19\frac{3}{4}$ in.)
Private Collection

Chronology

Compiled by *Katharina Schulz*
Translated by Anthony Vivis

1886

Oskar Kokoschka born 1 March at Pöchlarn, a small town on the Danube, about 100 km. west of Vienna; second of four children. 25 March: baptized a Catholic in the parish church at Pöchlarn. Father, Gustav Josef Kokoschka (1840–1923) from a Prague family of goldsmiths but now working as a 'travelling salesman' for a jewellery firm (entry in the parish register). Later finds a job in Vienna as a bookkeeper. Mother, Maria Romana Kokoschka, née Loidl (1861–1934) from a large family; her father a forester near Hollenstein in the Lower Austrian Alps.

1887

Family settles in Vienna, where their first son, Gustav, dies aged two and a half.

1889

Birth of OK's sister Berta, married name Patocková (1889–1960).

1892

Birth of his brother, Bohuslav (1892–1976).

OK starts at the local primary school. As an enrolment present, father gives him the 1835, four-language edition of *Orbis Sensualium Pictus*, written in 1658 by Johann Amos Comenius, the Moravian theologian and pedagogue. This humanist's educational ideas are later to become a guiding force in the artist's life.

During his school years, OK lives with his family on the outskirts of Vienna. Here 'the world was made up of a maze of gardens. Only a little further off fields and meadows began . . .' ('Aus meiner Jugendbiographie', *Der Wiener Kunstwanderer*, November 1933).

1895

Attends the Währinger Staatsrealschule, a secondary school specializing in modern languages, in Vienna's 18th District (Schopenhauerstrasse). Sings in the choir of the Piaristenkirche; its baroque ceiling paintings by Franz Anton Maulbertsch make a profound impression on him.

1904

Parents move to central Vienna (8, Helblinggasse; 17th District). After taking Matura ('A' Levels) at the Staatsrealschule OK initially wants to study chemistry. Through the good offices of his drawing-master, Johann Schober, awarded a State Scholarship to study at the *Kunstgewerbeschule* (School of Applied Arts) of the Austrian Museum for Art and Industry. 1 October: begins his studies, intending to qualify as a drawing-master at a secondary school.

Accordingly, enrols for the foundation course, under Anton von Kenner, and takes the following subjects: 'Course in Elementary and Figurative Drawing' under Erich von Mallina, 'Handwriting and Heraldry' (Rudolf von Larisch), 'Anatomical Drawing' (Hermann Heller), 'Stylistics' (Adolf Ginzel) and 'Art History' (Eduard Leisching). In first two years of study his efforts are generally considered 'very good' (mark of 2 in a scale descending from 1 to 5).

1906

In the library of the Museum of Applied Arts fascinated by Japanese woodcuts.

Spends the summer with the family of a maternal uncle Anton Loidl, at Lassing (on the Styrian frontier), where he sketches his immediate circle: cousin Julie, uncle, one of his uncle's brothers-in-law, and all these relatives at a family concert ('Chamber Music at Lassing'). Presumably at the same period produces his first portraits in oil, 'Juliana Loidl' and that of another cousin, 'Anna Donner', confirming his early interest in portraiture. In October, at the start of his third year of study, accepted by the *Fachschule für Malerei* (Faculty of Painting) whose director is Carl Otto Czeschka. Under Czeschka's tuition learns the techniques of printing from woodcuts and lithography; designs and executes *Ex libris*, posters and pictorial broadsheets. By the end of December is writing to his former English master: 'In my free time I paint absolutely as I like, and make quicker progress than I do in the studio with all its facilities' (to Leon Kellner, 31 December 1906) – here referring to the quick sketches he makes of models in motion, such as circus children found playing in the street.

1907

Czeschka leaves the School of Applied Arts, and for the next two years OK continues his studies under his successor, Berthold Löffler. With Löffler's help, becomes an associate of the *Wiener Werkstätte*, the design workshops founded by Josef Hoffmann, Koloman Moser and Fritz Waerndorfer in 1903 under the influence of the Arts and Crafts Movement. Most important project for the WW is the picture-book *Die Träumenden Knaben* (The Dreaming Youths), a commission from Waerndorfer. Starts work at the end of November, writing texts and illustrating them with eight coloured lithographs. Later describes the work as his first 'love letter', addressed to fellow student, Lilith Lang. In October the WW opens a theatre in central Vienna, the Cabaret Fledermaus, for which OK writes a fairy-tale, *The Speckled Egg*, and also makes special shadow puppets (performed 28

October). At the same time writes his first one-act play *Sphinx und Strohmann* (Sphinx and Strawman) and jots down ideas for *Mörder Hoffnung der Frauen* (Murderer Hope of Women).

1908

Parents move to 18, Breitenfeldergasse (8th District). OK produces drawings in pen, ink and gouache for *Der weisse Tiertöter* (The White Animal-Slayer), a sequel to *The Dreaming Youths*.

At the School of Applied Arts continues to work on projects for the WW (postcards, fans, vignettes and book decorations) and sketches the coloured lithograph 'Pietà' (published as a poster in 1909). Asked to take an evening class at the School, modified to suit his technique of drawing moving models. For this earns 300 crowns a month; together with his scholarship, his monthly income is 1100 crowns.

The *Kunstschau* 1908 offers him his first opportunity to show in public. Exhibition arranged jointly by the circle of artists around Gustav Klimt who have left the Vienna Secession, the WW and the School of Applied Arts. Held from May to September near the Schwarzenbergplatz. OK exhibits *The Dreaming Youths*, which in late June is published by the WW in an edition of 500 copies: his first literary publication, dedicated to

Klimt. Also shows three lifesize tapestry cartoons, *Die Traumtragenden* (The Dream-Bearers); ten drawings; a poster, *Die Baumwollpflückerin* (The Woman Cotton-Picker); and the sculpture of a girl. Most of his works are sold before the opening: Waerndorfer acquires the tapestry cartoons for 200 crowns, Emil Orlik and Kolo Moser buy his drawings. In reviews of the exhibition OK is the only one of the young artists to be mentioned; progressive critics are irritated, but admit he has talent, while conservative critics show a lack of understanding. Klimt calls OK 'the greatest talent of the younger generation'.

At the *Kunstschau* OK is introduced to the architect Adolf Loos. His friendship with Loos – particularly from 1909 onwards – becomes immensely important. Loos unselfishly promotes him whenever he can; arranges portrait commissions, and buys the pictures himself when they do not meet the subject's approval. Thanks to Loos, OK gets to know the liveliest minds in Vienna such as Karl Kraus, editor of the satirical magazine *Die Fackel* (The Torch), and the poet and essayist, Peter Altenberg. Inspired by the new ideas generated in Loos's circle, OK gradually moves away from the influence of the WW. In mid-October he accompanies Loos to Pudmaritz, where he paints his first landscape.

Woman Cotton-picker
(poster for the 1908 *Kunstschau*)

Kokoschka, summer 1909

1909

On 29 March the Cabaret Fledermaus presents a Kokoschka matinée with the motto 'I'm struggling for women'. Première of *Sphinx and Strawman* under the title *Groteskes Märchen* (A Grotesque Tale). Paints the portrait of his friend the actor Ernst Reinhold ('The Tranceplayer').

June: the 1st *Internationale Kunstschau* opens in Vienna. OK impressed by the works of Georges Minne, Munch, and Van Gogh. Represented by pen, ink and water-colour drawings for *The White Animal-Slayer*, and the portrait of Reinhold, as well as by nude studies, a painted fan and a sculpture – a self-portrait head in painted terracotta. The critic Ludwig Erik Tesar writes a longish appreciation of his works in the *Kunstrevue*. On 4 July *Murderer Hope of Women* and *Sphinx and Strawman* are performed in the open-air theatre at the *Kunstschau* by friends and fellow students from the School of Applied Arts. Paul Zinner composes the music. The press reacts with a mixture of amusement and incomprehension.

Under the influence of Van Gogh OK paints 'Still-life with Pineapple' and the portrait of 'Father Hirsch'.

At the end of the academic year, leaves the School of Applied Arts. In both of his final two years his work was consistently awarded the top mark: 'excellent'.

In his leaving certificate Löffler writes: 'Herr Oskar Kokoschka has an exceptionally versatile talent, and is extremely gifted both as a draughtsman and a painter. His works are very original in conception, powerful in expression, and extremely skilled in execution.'

Summer: Forms a close friendship with Loos, who encourages him to paint portraits. Loos has him kitted out by the Emperor's court tailor and in return OK paints the latter's portrait. Thanks to Loos is later introduced to the circle around the educationalist Dr Eugenie Schwarzwald and her economist husband. At the *Akademische Verband für Literatur und Musik* (Academic Association for Literature and Music) is introduced to the pioneers of modern music, Schoenberg, Berg and Webern. With Loos and Kraus, OK frequents the famous artists' rendezvous, the Café Central in the Herrengasse. The climate in Vienna gradually becomes too oppressive for him. By the end of August he is writing to a friend: 'I can't stand it here any longer, everything is as rigid as if no-one was ever heard to shout. All one's relationships follow deadly predictable lines, and the people are terribly stereotyped – like puppets . . . I often feel so gloomy that I cover myself in my quilt and scream, simply to do something real' (22 August 1908, to Erwin Lang).

In mid-August tries unsuccessfully to get a foothold in Munich, and possibly attempts to get his drawings accepted by the editors of *Jugend* and *Simplizissimus*. In Berlin, with the help of the musician and art journalist Herwarth Walden, Loos tries to make contact with Paul Cassirer, the well-known gallery owner, and Julius Meier-Graefe, one of the most highly regarded art critics, in order to arouse interest in OK's work. October: Paints portraits of Karl Kraus, Adolf Loos and Peter Altenberg.

Late December: accompanies Loos to Switzerland. In the sanatorium at Les Avants, they visit Loos's mistress the English dancer, Bessie Bruce.

1910

January: From a window in the Grand Hôtel at Les Avants paints the view of the Gramont, opposite. This picture, which has become famous as 'Les Dents du Midi', is bought by Alfred Flechtheim, a collector from Düsseldorf. In the middle of the month, at Yvorne, paints the natural scientist, Auguste Forel. By the end of the month he is at Leysin, in the Sanatorium Mont Blanc, where Loos and Bessie have moved in the meantime. Paints the portraits of Bessie Bruce, Conte Verona and the Montesquiou-Fezensačs.

February: returns to Vienna. Introduced to Walden, who has come to discuss with Kraus his projected new magazine *Der Sturm* (The Storm). In the *Fackel* the first detailed critique of Kokoschka's work appears (21 March, L.E. Tesar, 'Oskar Kokoschka: a Conversation').

March: Probably short visit to Berlin. Stays at Walden's house and while there works as an associate editor on the *Sturm*. Makes plans with Walden for further co-operation. During the next few years the periodical develops into Germany's leading organ of the international avant-garde, in the fine arts as well as in literature. OK makes a significant contribution to its content and design. Between May and December his pen and ink drawings appear regularly. By the middle of the year, as part of the series *Menschenköpfe* (People's Heads), portrait drawings of Kraus, Loos and Walden, among others, have also appeared.

The publication of *Murderer Hope of Women* in the *Sturm*, with illustrations specially created for it, has a stimulating effect on virtually all early Expressionist dramatic writing in Germany. OK's drawings arouse a lot of interest among avant-garde artists. Oskar Schlemmer visits Berlin in 1910 and sends the first issues to his friends at the Stuttgart Academy. 'Also at that time the first of Oskar Kokoschka's drawings to come to our attention

appeared in the *Sturm*. To us in Stuttgart, the drawings in each eagerly awaited issue seemed to shake the edifice of modern art like earth tremors. The dramatic effect these "sensations" had on our group simply cannot be over-stressed. My circle included the painters Oskar Schlemmer, Willi Baumeister and Paul Bollmann – and even the austere Otto Meyer-Amden got excited . . .' (Memoirs of Gustav Schleicher). And Kandinsky tells Marc about the 'very good Kokoschkas' in the *Sturm* (27 April 1912).

Probably in April OK returns to Vienna. Meets the collector Oskar Reichel, who right up to 1916 regularly buys pictures from him. In Reichel's house paints 'Still-life with Tortoise, Lamb and Hyacinth' and the portrait of Reichel's son Hans.

By the end of May back in Berlin helping to prepare his first big exhibition at Paul Cassirer's gallery. Paints the portrait of Walden.

June: Opening of his exhibition at the Cassirer gallery. Together with works by the young Hans Hofmann, OK shows twenty-seven oils, eight illustrations to *The White Animal-Slayer*, and drawings of nudes. The Berlin press fails to respond, with only the *Sturm* publishing reviews, including one by Walden's wife, the poet Else Lasker-Schüler.

Karl Ernst Osthaus, director of the Folkwang Museum, Hagen, discovers OK's works at Cassirer's and asks if he can show them in an exhibition at Hagen. In August the Folkwang Museum holds OK's first one-man show. Subsequently, Osthaus purchases the portrait of the Duchess of Montesquiou for 800 marks – the first museum purchase of a Kokoschka oil.

In the first week of August travels with Walden and Lasker-Schüler to the Rhineland, visiting Bonn, Düsseldorf (5 August), Cologne (6 August) and Elberfeld, to drum up support for the *Sturm*.

In Berlin OK leads a restless Bohemian life. In Walden's house (5, Katharinenstrasse) shares an attic room with the actor Rudolf Blümner. With Walden frequents the famous Café des Westens on the Kurfürstendamm (now the Café Kranzler), also called the 'Café Grössenwahn' (Café Megalomania), a rendezvous for poets, musicians, painters and actors. Paints portraits of Blümner, the director and sculptor William Wauer and the writers Paul Scheerbart and Peter Baum. Becomes interested in the works of Strindberg and Richard Dehmel; makes a drawing of the latter, and also wants to paint him, 'because I can make a better job of it than Liebermann'.

Shows a strong inclination to *épater le bourgeois*: the artist George Grosz remembers a ball 'where Kokoschka appeared with a real ox-bone dripping

blood, which he gnawed at from time to time'. Or he would sit in the Berlin Panoptikum among waxworks of the most notorious criminals, and suddenly leap out threateningly to terrify visitors. By the end of the year, the uncertainty and restlessness of his life in Berlin are such that he writes to a friend in Vienna: 'By now I'm so weak I can't fool myself any longer . . . I long to get back to Vienna . . . my whole life is hellish . . . and [I] am a bad-tempered weakling desperate for any sympathy that comes my way' (to Lotte Franzos, 24 December 1910).

1911

In January OK leaves Berlin, presumably having first talked to Walden about future sales of his pictures. Accuses his former friend the Viennese painter Max Oppenheimer of plagiarizing his work. In order to forestall an Oppenheimer exhibition travels to Munich and Salzburg: 'Up to now I've had nothing but failures; I had a row with Wedekind – he was behaving like a megalomaniac and I was rude. All the exhibition sites are taken, so that my friend Oppenheimer will inform the Munich public about my art before I do . . .' (to Lotte Franzos, undated). In the *Sturm* Lasker-Schüler writes a malicious 'Letter to an Imitator' attacking Oppenheimer.

In February the *Hagenbund* in Vienna opens an exhibition of contemporary art from Austria, Germany and Switzerland. Among those represented are Anton Faistauer, Karl Hofer and Bernhard Hoetger. OK's works form a focal point of the exhibition: twenty-five oils including the portraits of Altenberg, Loos and Kraus, as well as ten nude drawings. The conservative press reacts fiercely: his pictures are described as 'repulsive plague-sores' and 'phantoms of a morbid youth'. The *Fackel* and the *Sturm*, however, print enthusiastic reviews. The *Hagenbund* is OK's last exhibition in Vienna until 1924.

After his return from Berlin stays at his parents' house at 18, Breitenfeldergasse. Paints 'Hermann Schwarzwald I' in whose house he is a frequent guest. Begins a sequence of biblical pictures including 'Knight, Death and Angel I' and 'The Annunciation'.

Start of lifelong friendship with the poet Albert Ehrenstein, whose book, *Tubutsch*, he illustrates. Again paints people in his immediate circle, the actor Karl Etlinger, the composer and musicologist Egon Wellesz and the Baron Viktor von Dirsztay. Works on a play which initially he calls *Schauspiel* but later changes to *Der brennende Dornbusch* (The Burning Bush).

From 1 July to 15 August his second one-man show, consisting of twenty-nine oils, is held at

Karlsbad. In the autumn starts work as a drawing-master at the girls' school in Vienna founded by Eugenie Schwarzwald. Teaches the second class (fifth form) for three hours a week. Inspired by Franz Cizek's tuition at the School of Applied Arts, OK encourages his pupils to paint from their imagination instead of making academic copies.

In late autumn, thanks to Schoenberg and Loos, comes into contact with the artists of the *Blaue Reiter*. Kandinsky, Marc and Gabriele Münter work on the publication of an almanac, which appears in May, 1912. In it, Kokoschka's portrait 'Else Kupfer' is reproduced as an example of modern art. Münter writes to Schoenberg (27 September 1911) asking for Kokoschka's address; Kandinsky writes to Marc: 'Loos and Kokoschka are on our side' (22 December 1911).

1912
OK's works are becoming known abroad. In January the *Künstlerhaus* in Budapest exhibits works by modern Austrian artists, including Egon Schiele, Schoenberg and OK (three portraits). On 12 March at 34a, Tiergartenstrasse, Berlin, Walden opens the first exhibition at his new *Sturm* gallery (March–April). Alongside works by *Blaue Reiter* artists and other Expressionists, OK is represented by six oils, thirty-nine drawings, a poster and a relief.

Eugenie Schwarzwald, c. 1930

At the third *Sturm* exhibition in May, 42 of his drawings are shown. The *Grosse Kunstausstellung* in Dresden (1 May–15 October) includes a new religious painting 'The Visitation'; and at the epoch-making *International Exhibition of the Sonderbund* in Cologne (25 May–29 September) he is represented by six oils. The Wallraf-Richartz Museum in Cologne subsequently acquires the picture 'Les Dents du Midi' for 1,800 gold marks. In a critique of the *Sonderbund* Exhibition, Paul Ferdinand Schmidt describes OK as the 'first Viennese one can call a genius'.

On 26 January at the Academic Association for Music and Literature gives a lecture *Vom Bewusstsein der Gesichte* (On the Nature of Visions). There are 'noisy demonstrations' whereupon the higher educational authorities demand his 'immediate dismissal' from the Schwarzwald School (notice of dismissal dated 11 May).

On 12 or 15 April 1912 meets Alma Mahler, step-daughter of the painter Carl Moll, and widow of the composer Gustav Mahler. Start of a passionate romance, which temporarily alienates the artist from Loos and his friends. The excitement and intensity of this relationship are reflected in his letters and works; during the next few years the figure of Alma Mahler becomes the leitmotif of his paintings, lithographs and drawings. Writes to Alma: 'You

Alma Mahler

have so enhanced me that I can no longer remember what I once was, you most noble of women . . . Before, I was old, tired to death, and almost imbecilic . . . And now I'm a joyful, young God who longs to shoulder gigantic burdens only to toss them away with a laugh when you come to me, my Only One, my Eternal Love' (To AM, 8 May 1912).

During the summer works on portrait commissions in Vienna; and at Semmering (in the Eastern Austrian Alps) from 13 July to 22 July. In August travels with Alma to Switzerland, visiting Mürren and Lauterbrunnen (13–late August). Paints 'Alpine Landscape, Mürren' and a portrait of Alma, which he finishes 6 December 1912. At the end of August – for the first time ever – signs a contract with an art dealer which enables him to send home 400 crowns a month and keep 'adequate pocket-money for his personal needs'. By this means he hopes to free himself from the 'wearing, extremely enervating commercial connections with coffee-house friends and private individuals in Vienna, to whom one is forever indebted. I now desperately need a period of time when I can work without worries, so that I can develop my abilities and not be held back by painting for money . . . Now I must get proper recognition abroad' (mid-August, to his mother). The dealer is presumably the Berlin gallery owner Wolfgang Gurlitt, who plans to publish a portfolio of OK's lithographs.

In September, travels to western Germany (15 September in Baden-Baden). In Frankfurt, at the *Blaue Reiter* Exhibition, introduced to Franz Marc and his wife; Marc subsequently writes to Gabriele Münter that 'both as an artist and a personality Kokoschka is absolutely one of us' (14 November 1912). In Cologne sees the *Sonderbund* Exhibition. At the end of September returns to Vienna. 1 October: Starts teaching at the School of Applied Arts as assistant to Professor Kenner. For ten hours a week gives classes in 'general life drawing'; attendance is voluntary and his students learn to draw models in motion. Earns 1,800 crowns a year from this work, and stays for one academic year.

1913
Almost always in financial difficulties, as he is also supporting his family. Runs up debts, asks Walden for advances, and – presumably in violation of his commitments to Walden – sells pictures to other dealers. From 1913 on, the Viennese private collector Franz Hauer, the Mannheim businessman Falk and the Hanover collector Herbert Garvens-Garvensburg acquire his pictures.

The 'Double-portrait (Oskar Kokoschka and Alma Mahler)' finished in March, is meant to depict their engagement. They make plans for their future together; Alma has a house built at Semmering. In March they travel to Italy, visiting Venice, Naples (20 March–10 April) and Pompeii (8 April). In Venice OK admires Titian's painting, but above all works by Tintoretto. At the beginning of April, paints the Bay of Naples.

Returning to Vienna (10 April), he now – not, as was previously assumed, in 1914 – starts work on the painting which has since become famous as 'Die Windsbraut' (The Tempest). Writes to Alma: 'Slowly – but with constant improvements – the picture advances toward completion. The two of us with very strong, calm expressions, clasping each other's hands, framed by a semi-circle of sea lit up by fireworks, a water-tower, mountains, lightning, and the moon. Until the mass of small details once more resolved themselves into the idea I originally had, and I was able to express the mood I wanted by reliving it – what it means to make a promise! Despite all the turmoil in the world, to know that one person can put eternal trust in another, that two people can be committed to themselves and other people by an act of faith' (To AM, April 1913).

With Ernst Reinhold rehearses the production of his drama *Schauspiel* for the *Neue Wiener Bühne* (New Viennese Stage); on 2 June, after the censor declares it 'offensive to public morals', the performance is cancelled. Nevertheless the play is published together with *Murderer Hope of Women* and *Sphinx and Strawman* in the first monograph on the now 27-year-old artist, *Oskar Kokoschka: Dramen und Bilder*, with an introduction by Paul Stefan.

At the end of June leaves the School of Applied Arts. Works on twelve lithographs for *Der Gefesselte Kolumbus* (Columbus in Chains), which reflects the tensions in his affair with Alma Mahler.

In late August, travels with Alma to the Dolomites (from 22 August). On the way, stays at Schluderbach and Misurina.

From the Hotel Tre Croci paints the view towards the mountain range Tre Croci. Late September, after his return to Vienna, moves into a new studio at 27, Hardtgasse, which he keeps until 1915.

In mid-November pays a brief visit to Berlin (15 November Hotel Botania, Potsdamerstrasse) for discussions with Walden and Gurlitt. Visits the *Erste Deutscher Herbstsalon* (First German Autumn Salon) organized by Walden, featuring paintings of the international avant-garde. At the end of the year completes 'Die Windsbraut', a title supplied by the poet Georg Trakl during a visit to his studio. 'The picture is an event . . . my strongest and greatest piece of work, the masterpiece of all Expressionist endeavours' (to Walden, December 1913).

OK's pictures are now exhibited in several major European cities, including Budapest, Zurich, Munich and Stuttgart. In the New Year, thanks to Cassirer's initiative, four oils are shown at the 26th Exhibition of the Berlin Secession. Subsequently, the Kunsthalle Mannheim purchases the portrait of Auguste Forel for 1,100 gold marks, and the Hanover collector Garven-Garvensburg acquires the double-portrait of Alma and Oskar.

1914

Spends most of the spring with Alma Mahler at Semmering. Alma is pregnant, but has an abortion in a Viennese clinic. OK paints 'Still-life with Putto and Rabbit'. In March completes the dramatic poem begun in 1913, *Wehmann und Windsbraut* (The Man of Sorrows and The Tempest), published in 1915 under the title *Allos makar* (Happy in a Different Way). These verses, like the eleven lithographs he produces soon afterwards for *Bach Cantata: O Ewigkeit Du Donnerwort* (Eternity Thou Fearful Word), again evoke his turbulent relationship with Alma.

In March, Kurt Wolff in Leipzig publishes *Die Chinesische Mauer* (The Great Wall of China) by Karl Kraus, with eight lithographs by OK, in an edition of 200 copies. Paints portraits of friends and acquaintances, including Franz Hauer and Ehrenstein (April). Makes several plans to paint frescoes and asks Walden for help: 'Couldn't you get me a commission for fresco work in America? I'm ripe for work of this kind – which is my true vocation, but I'm forced to go on daubing small-scale pictures which are bound to be unsatisfactory to me' (To Walden, 28 April). Over the fireplace in Alma's house at Semmering paints a fresco whose subject is the two lovers (May). At the same time commissioned to paint murals for a crematorium to be built at Breslau by Max Berg. Goes to Breslau for consultations with the architect (25 May) and completes colour sketches.

In late June spends three days in Berlin, where he works at a printers on the lithographs for *Bach Cantata*. On 28 June the Austro-Hungarian Crown Prince, Franz Ferdinand, is assassinated at Sarajevo by Serbian conspirators, and a month later Austria-Hungary declares war on Serbia. OK writes to Kurt Wolff: 'If I were able to earn enough money to keep my relatives' heads above water, I would happily volunteer for the army, because anyone who stays at home will never live down the shame' (late September). Through Ludwig von Ficker, editor of the Innsbruck periodical *Der Brenner*, given a 5,000 crown grant from the Ludwig Wittgenstein Foundation (6 November). Shortly afterwards enlists for military service. With Loos's

help assigned to the cavalry – the 15th Imperial-Royal Regiment of Dragoons, one of the most prestigious in the Dual Monarchy. The last picture he completes before joining up is 'Knight Errant'.

Summer: Achieves a great success with 'The Tempest' at the exhibition of the New Munich Secession. The Munich critic Wilhelm Hausenstein considers it the most important work in the exhibition. 'Seldom has the visionary element in recent art . . . been expressed with such . . . a convincing vigour of observation' (*Kunstchronik*, 21 August 1914). The Hamburg pharmacist Otto Winter buys the picture for 4,000 crowns (8 December).

1915

On 3 January, begins his military training at Wiener Neustadt, about 40 miles south of Vienna. Lives in the Hotel Central. Persistent financial worries. The Wittgenstein Foundation gives him another grant, of 700 crowns (6 February). Acquires a horse, which he christens 'Minden Lo'. Reports to his mother a typical day: '7–7.30: horseback riding, exercises in infantry combat, squadron exercises, 10–11: marching into barracks . . . field exercises with enemy forces and bullets – with me on patrol, also climbing up and down mountains, learning how to crawl on all fours, and

Kokoschka in the uniform of a dragoon, 1915

digging – until 12.30 p.m. An hour's meal break, then at 2 o'clock: stable inspection, 2.30: marching out of barracks or target-practice, at which I've never hit anything . . . 4.30: marching into barracks, parade in the barrack square to be given orders, and listen to duties, punishments etc. being read out. I've already had two lots of 24 hour guard duty' (late January/early February); and to Alma writes: 'Since I am on duty the whole day in the snow, I have given up all hope of being able to do my work and live off it' (late January).

Alma breaks up with OK and begins a new relationship with the architect Walter Gropius (February). At the beginning of March field exercises in Bruck, near Wiener Neustadt (2–5 March). During April and May given further training in Holič, where he volunteers for the Front, in order to avoid the threat of arrest after being guilty of insubordination. Returns to Wiener Neustadt. In mid-July sent to the Eastern Front, to Galicia, and on 22 July arrives at Lemberg. As a cadet-sergeant, mobilized in the Eastern Ukraine as a patrol-rider (from 25 July).

Reports to his friend Ehrenstein: 'A few days ago I survived a dangerous skirmish on horseback with some Cossacks . . . We lost five out of our nine men. I was the last to flee, because my horse became a little lame in the marsh, and those devils were constantly on my tail with their spears and their cries of "Urrah-Urrah". But I kept my head, and having got away safely I feel insanely happy . . . I've been made a cadet' (8 August 1915). 18 August: in Berlin Alma marries Gropius.

After 29 August, near Luck in the Western Ukraine, OK is badly wounded by a bullet in the head and a bayonet thrust in the lung. Newspapers in Vienna announce his death. After a few days in a field hospital on 3 September he is taken to Brünn (now Brno, about 150 km from Vienna). In hospital at Brünn conceives his drama *Orpheus and Eurydice*, in which his love for Alma and the end of their relationship is expressed in mythical images.

In mid-October transferred to the infirmary at the Palais Palffy in Vienna, where remains till February 1916.

The third volume of Meier-Graefe's *History of the Development of Modern Art* contains a chapter on OK. In August shown for the first time in the U.S.A. in the exhibition *Oil-paintings from Austrian and Hungarian Private Collections* at San Francisco. Loos makes his collection of Kokoschkas available for it.

1916

Oskar Reichel buys 'Knight Errant'.

On release from hospital (February) declared unfit for military service for three months. Lives with his parents, at 8, Bennoplatz; temporarily mobilized as an inspection officer at various infirmaries in Vienna and Klosterneuburg, and subsequently in the military press office.

Paints the specialist attending him, Heinrich von Neumann and the group portrait 'Prince Dietrichstein and Family'. The young Alexandrine, Duchess Mensdorff-Dietrichstein takes an interest in the invalid, and they go for coach

rides in the Weidlingau Park, near Vienna. Introduced to the poet Rainer Maria Rilke, whom he often meets.

In mid-July ordered to serve as a liaison officer on the Isonzo Front (the Slovenian-Italian theatre of war). Writes to Ehrenstein, who is trying to arrange for his works to be sold and published in Berlin: 'I'm staying on here for another five days, then on the 14th I have to start the journey with some war artists, which I am dreading and which I am sure will very soon cost me my life . . . I'm already sick to death of life, and I'm waiting for the end of the world, when I hope I'll be able to find a cleft in the ground where I can rest' (10 July 1916). Accompanies a group of war artists by way of Klagenfurt (17 July) and Laibach to Tolmino (21 July). 'I'm group leader and I'm directly responsible for everything, the artists' work, their conduct, travel arrangements, food, etc. to the local High Command' (to his mother, 17 July 1916). Draws and paints landscapes and portraits at the Front. In several letters repeatedly asks Walden to look around for a professorship for him. In late August a grenade which goes off very near him contributes to shell-shock; taken to a military hospital in Vienna.

On 9 September in Berlin. Stays at the Hotel Central and rents a studio. Frequent visits to the Kaiser-Friedrich-Museum. Paints portraits of Nell Walden, Walden's second wife, and of Princess Mechthild Lichnowsky. Works on six lithographs for *The Passion*, which are published by Cassirer in the yearbook *Der Bildermann*. In Berlin the Fritz Gurlitt Verlag publishes his portfolios *Columbus in*

Kokoschka in Galicia, 1915

Kokoschka convalescing, Vienna, early 1916

Chains and *Bach Cantata*.

Tries to secure a professorship at Dresden, and spends a short time there (mid-September). Between 13 September and 19 September in Berlin, where he signs a contract with Walden. Writes to his parents: 'On the positive side, signed a contract which for three years gives me a regular monthly income of 2,000 marks, for which I have to complete 10 drawings per month and 12 oil paintings per year... In Dresden I have surprisingly good prospects of getting through the professorial appointment board without much opposition, and being given the job. The Rector is for me, and has no candidate of his own, four *Hofräte* are making strenuous efforts to convince the professors, and the *Stadtbaurat* is a friend of Berg's in Breslau and will plead my cause. Let us hope to God that this venture, which would solve all my difficulties in more ways than one, will turn out successfully. Dresden is exquisitely beautiful, all being well I think you could all move here' (19 September). In fact, however, the decision on the professorship is postponed until the end of the war.

In late October concludes a new contract, this time with Cassirer. To his parents: 'I'm dissolving the other contract, amicably I hope, in the New Year. At the time I did need it, though, because Cassirer will only jump to it if someone else has already taken a risk' (22 October). The new contract contains the following stipulations (according to the artist):

'1. O.K. has unconditional freedom as to the number and frequency of works to be completed for Cassirer during the contractual year.

2. O.K. agrees to pass all commissions on to Cassirer, and to accept new ones only with Cassirer's approval, who takes a 25% share of any proceeds.

3. Accounts to be settled every six months.

4. Graphic works subject to separate calculations.

5. Cassirer agrees to pay Kokoschka a guaranteed monthly sum of 2,500 marks (minimum sum).' (Letter to his parents, 23 October 1916). This business agreement with Cassirer gives OK financial security, with a few interruptions, until 1931.

November: works on the drama *Orpheus and Eurydice*, and presumably at this time also paints the picture of the same name. In Leipzig introduced to the painter Max Klinger. 'It was almost as if the older Goethe was coming towards me. So old and so young and so engaging ... We drained two bottles of red wine' (to his sister, 16 November 1916).

Wishes to avoid another call-up for active service, since '... in that case, if I was lucky, I would have to work as a war artist out in the open, which I'd find far too dangerous and monotonous. After I've come through so much safe and sound, I don't want to get killed now the War's nearly over' (to his mother, 26 November 1916). With Ehrenstein's help, on 1 December, sent to convalesce in Dr Teuscher's sanatorium in the Weisser Hirsch district of Dresden, where 'I also have friends among the doctors, who will give me refuge for as long as possible'. Meets Dr Fritz Neuberger. At the Felsenburg Inn, Weisser Hirsch, introduced to the actor Ernst Deutsch from Prague, the Expressionist dramatist Walter Hasenclever and the poet Ivan von

Lücken, whom he sees frequently. Becomes friendly with the actress Käthe Richter, who from 1916 to 1918 is engaged by the Albert Theatre in Dresden. Starts work on the picture 'The Exiles' in which Richter, Neuberger and OK are depicted. In winter, at the sanatorium, paints 'Landscape in Saxony'.

The Munich Staatsgalerie acquires the picture 'Tre Croci'. OK contributes to several group exhibitions e.g. the *Wiener Kunstschau* held, on Paul Cassirer's initiative, at the Berlin Secession premises (232, Kurfürstendamm), from 8 January to 20 February (three portraits, two landscapes, and 'The Visitation'). In April Walden organizes the 40th *Sturm* Exhibition, *Oskar Kokoschka and Otokar Kubin*, with 'The Tempest' as its focal point. In Dresden contributes to an exhibition of the *Künstlervereinigung* (Artists' Association) founded in 1912, which includes works by Beckmann, Lehmbruck, Pechstein and Schiele.

1917

OK is frequently ill, suffering a disturbance to his sense of balance as a result of war wounds. Works on his third drama *Hiob* (Job), an expanded version of *Sphinx and Strawman*, which reflects his depressed state. The theme is once again the agonies of man-woman relationships. On 14 April, the première of this first revised version takes place at the Dada Gallery in Zurich, under Marcel Janco's direction; Hugo Ball and Tristan Tzara play the main parts. Simultaneously, the Dada Gallery exhibits pictures by OK, Max Ernst, Klee and Kandinsky. The

Kokoschka and his brother Bohuslav (left), Vienna, early 1916

Job, Albert Theatre, Dresden, June 1917

third and final version of the play called *Sphinx and Strawman II* or *Job* is given its première on 3 June at the Albert Theatre, Dresden, together with *Murderer Hope of Women* and *The Burning Bush*. OK directs and designs the production himself, with Käthe Richter and Ernst Deutsch taking the main parts. In the *Kunstblatt* (Art Journal) Camill Hoffmann writes a rave review ('Oskar Kokoschka's Poetry and Plays') the first appreciation of OK as a dramatist. The Paul Cassirer publishing house issues a book-edition of *Job* with fourteen lithographs by the artist. In Leipzig, as part of the series *Der jüngste Tag* (The Day of Judgment), Kurt Wolff publishes *The Burning Bush* and *Murderer Hope of Women*.

In March completes 'The Exiles'. Paints 'Lovers with Cat', which depicts Käthe Richter and Hasenclever. Produces a number of important drawings and lithographs, including the portraits of Neuberger, Richter and Hasenclever, as well as the satirical drawings 'Soldiers, Fighting Each Other with Crucifixes', and 'Peace Among Nations' (summer). The latter mark OK's first confrontation with political events. Paul Westheim publishes a longish article on 'The Painter Oskar Kokoschka' in *Das Kunstblatt*.

1 August: the Foreign Ministry in Vienna invites OK to contribute to the exhibition *Modern Austrian Art* at Stockholm, which is being held in conjunction with the International Peace Congress. Given a travel permit by the military High Command in Vienna and in mid-September travels to Stockholm by train and boat via Berlin, Sassnitz and Trelleborg. Lives in a hotel at 3, Nybrogatan. Since his Berlin days in 1910, OK has been an admirer of the works of Strindberg and Ibsen; around 1916/17 reads the novel *Pan* by the Norwegian writer Knut Hamsun, which is to remain one of his favourite books all his life. Identifies with the character of Lieutenant Glahn, the hero of the novel, a demobilized soldier, who can't adjust to an alien environment, is torn between the love of two women, and ends up losing both and destroying himself (OK later signs several letters 'Lieutenant Glahn').

With the help of Stefan Grossmann, editor of the *Vossische Zeitung* in Berlin, probably gains access to the speeches and debates at the International Peace Congress. His impressions are set down in the short story 'Letter from Stockholm' (Winter 1917): 'Despite all the talk about peace conferences in Stockholm, I realised in the first few days that no such thing could ever be held successfully in such a place because sympathy for the suffering decreases the further you get from that part of Europe which is tearing itself apart.'

Makes drawings of the Mayor of Stockholm, Carl Lindhagen, the Nobel Prize Winner Svanthe Arrhenius, and in Marbåcka (Varmland Province) of the poetess Selma Lagerlöf (late September). Paints 'Stockholm Harbour' (October) with a view of Strandvägen, and in it he fulfils the resolution he made in the trenches, that should he survive he would henceforth paint only from the highest possible viewpoint 'in order to show what Europe still has to offer'.

Frequent visits to the National Museum in Stockholm. Discovers the Swedish painter Ernst Josephson (late nineteenth century) and stands admiringly in front of Rembrandt's 'The Conspiracy of Claudius Civilius' of 1661. On 24 October writes to Ehrenstein: 'I'm even more wretched than ever . . . on top of everything I have to spend at least two or three days a week in bed, with a high fever; my lung simply can't take the strain any more, I get hellish chest-pains, and I feel quite certain that my strength and youth are gone – not to mention my health.' Through Ragnar Hoppe, an assistant at the National Museum in Stockholm, goes to Upsala to consult Professor Bárány, the Austrian physiologist and Nobel Prize Winner. Bárány gives him a medical certificate to show the authorities he is unfit for military service.

21 November: returns to the Weisser Hirsch, Dresden. Asks Kurt Wolff in Leipzig to support his case at the Darmstädter Hof for a professorship at the Academy there. Starts work on the oil-painting 'The Friends', which depicts Richter, Hasenclever, von Lücken, Neuberger and himself. Gives the following description in a letter to Hans Tietze: 'It shows my friends, playing cards. Each one absorbed in his own passion, frighteningly naked, and each one of them steeped in colour of a higher intensity, which binds them all together like light connecting an object and its mirror-image, raising them to a level that combines qualities of its real appearance with those of its reflection, leaving both intensified as a result.'

April: contributes to an exhibition at the Dada Gallery in Zurich. Exhibits two pictures in the Berlin *Free Secession* (1 July–30 September). In Zurich represented at the group exhibition *German Painters of the 19th and 20th Centuries* (Kunsthaus). The Städel in Frankfurt purchases the portrait 'Dr. Schwarzwald I' for 800 marks. Cassirer starts to publish the great portrait-lithographs ('Romana Kokoschka', 'Dr. Fritz Neuberger', 'Käthe Richter').

1918

Continues to provide for his family; for two years starting from 1 February pays a monthly sum of 300 marks in order to clear a debt he incurred in 1913 to provide his sister with her trousseau. Finishes his fourth drama *Orpheus and Eurydice* (January-February), illustrating the text with six etchings for an edition planned by the Dresden photographer Hugo Erfurth (which does not materialize). Completes 'The Friends'. Shaken by the deaths of Gustav Klimt (6 February) and Fritz Neuberger (17 May). Visited in Dresden by his father and sister (July); Kokoschka draws his father (lithograph 'Gustav Kokoschka').

Summer: Meets the doll-maker Hermine Moos from Munich. OK commissions her to make him a life-size doll in the likeness of Alma Mahler, to look as lifelike as possible, around 35–40 years old with hair a 'golden chestnut-red'. Asks Moos 'to carry out this project to my satisfaction, creating so convincing a magic that I shall believe when I see and touch the woman of my dreams I have made her come to life.' Moos continues working on the doll until spring 1919. (Letters of 22 July and 20 August.)

November/December: First one-man show at Cassirer's Gallery in Berlin, consisting of thirty paintings, including 'The Friends'.

In Berlin experiences the November Revolution at first hand (short story 'Jessica') and comes into contact with the artists of the *Novembergruppe* (November Group) who welcome the revolution. However, at the first session of the November Group on 3 December sends his apologies for absence and asks for his name not to be mentioned in the press. After his return (11 December) to Dresden produces the coloured lithograph 'The Principle' with the inscription 'Liberté, Egalité, Fratricide'.

In December moves into the Felsenburg Inn at the Weisser Hirsch. Works on the paintings 'The Pagans' and 'The Power of Music'. Introduced to Dr. Hans Posse, director of the Dresden Gemäldegalerie. Towards the end of the year Paul Westheim's monograph appears in print (54 pp, with 62 illustrations). The Viennese art historian Hans Tietze publishes an essay on OK in the *Zeitschrift für bildende Kunst* (Journal of the Fine Arts). Fritz Gurlitt publishes the *Bach Cantata* as a portfolio (second edition) as well as in book form, with eleven lithographs in each case.

Exhibitions: January – declines Egon Schiele's invitation to collaborate with the Vienna Secession, since he has no wish 'to feel at home there ever again even with the most minor of my works' (6 January).

1919

The post-1918 years are more turbulent in Dresden than in many other German cities, since with the fall of the monarchy it loses its centuries-old status as a *Residenzstadt*. OK is restless and depressed and feels alien in revolutionary Germany (short story 'Dresden' 1919–20). By the beginning of April the doll is ready. OK wants it to keep him company since – as he writes to Moos – he 'cannot tolerate any living human beings, [but] on his own is often a prey to despair' (10 December 1918). On seeing the finished product, however, he is horrified, since it in no way fulfils his high expectations. By June has completed several drawings of the doll, and paints 'Woman in Blue'. Finally, after a night with friends drinking champagne, throws it on to a Dresden refuse-lorry (probably summer 1920).

25 May: productions of *The Burning Bush* and *Job* at Max Reinhardt's *Kammerspieltheater* in Berlin, with OK directing: the first performance of any of his plays in Berlin. In *Das junge Deutschland* Heinz Herald writes about the 'Kokoschka Scandal'. Cassirer publishes the four dramas *Murderer Hope of Women*, *Job*, *The Burning Bush* and *Orpheus and Eurydice*.

From June, back in Dresden, OK works on the double-portrait of his friends Carl Georg Heise and Hans Mardersteig. 18 August: Ministry of the Interior sends him a contract for the professorship at the Dresden Academy, to run for seven years at an annual salary of 4,800 marks, plus 540 marks accommodation expenses. Teaching duties begin on 1 October. In the autumn, in his new studio at the Brühlsche-Terrasse above the River Elbe, paints the first of his Elbe views, 'Dresden, Neustadt I'. Apart from OK, the teaching staff at the Academy includes Otto Gussmann, Hans Poelzig and Karl Albiker. From 1919 to 1920 Otto Dix is a master student under Max Feldbauer. When later that year Dix and the writer Konrad Felixmüller found the Dresden Secession, they make OK honorary member. OK's students include Hans Meyboden, Joachim Heuer and Willy Kriegel.

In December, moves in with Dr. Hans Posse, to occupy one of the 8 *Kavaliershäuschen* (lodges) in the park of the Dresden Residenz. The Dresden Gemäldegalerie acquires 'The Power of Music', completed in the summer.

1920

March: in an exchange of fire during the Kapp Putsch (15 March) a Rubens picture in the Old Master collection at the Dresden Zwinger is damaged. Subsequently, OK writes an appeal 'To the People of Dresden', which he has distributed in the streets and published in over forty daily German papers, in protest against the destruction of cultural assets by revolutionary commandos. In Berlin George Grosz and John Heartfield publicly criticize him for this, calling him an 'artistic thug' (*Kunstlump*). OK writes to his parents: 'The Germans are like that – they are quite prepared to kill each other out of sheer obstinacy. They don't have eyes, just ideas – which bear no relation to reality' (31 March). Works on a new 'large painting', possibly the 'Self-portrait with Easel':

'Now at last the sun is shining and I myself feel extremely energetic and hopeful: I now believe that with this new picture I shall succeed in painting something which will do German art of the future a great service' (31 March). The city of Dresden purchases 'The Pagans'.

Spring: Holds frequent classes in the Dresden Gemäldegalerie in front of pictures by Caspar David Friedrich, Vermeer and Van Eyck. His teaching methods in the Academy are unusual, 'like a fresh breeze, full of turbulence and one surprise after another' (F.K. Gotsch).

April: Productions of *Job* and *Murderer Hope of Women* (11 April) in the *Neue Theater* Frankfurt, with Heinrich George, Gerda Müller and Carl Zeistig. The writer Carl Zuckmayer reports that the performance ends in a brawl. It is slated in the *Frankfurter Zeitung*: 'Any more of this sort of thing and culturally Germany is finished' (12 April).

From mid-June in Vienna. Takes leave of absence from the Academy in Dresden and stays for seven months. With financial help from Cassirer, buys his family a house on the outskirts of the city, at 29 Liebhartstalstrasse (16th District). In the house of the art historian Karl Maria Swoboda produces a series of drawings of Camilla Swoboda, listening to her husband playing the piano.

August: Moves with his family into the Liebhartstal house.

Autumn/Winter: In the Cassirer Yearbook for 1920 his essay 'Vorrede zum *Orbis pictus*' (Prologue to the *Orbis Pictus*) appears; written in 1919 under the immediate impact of the turmoil of war, this is an indictment of the senseless butchery of the First World War.

The composer Paul Hindemith scores *Murderer Hope of Women* as an opera.

1921

On 17 January returns to Dresden, where he leads a boisterous life and is generally known as the 'crazy Kokoschka'.

February: in Frankfurt on 2 February for the première of his play *Orpheus and Eurydice* in the *Schauspielhaus* under the direction of Heinrich George.

In Dresden a prolific period of creativity begins. Paints 'Saul and David' and two more Elbe views from his studio window ('Dresden, Neustadt II' and 'III'). Writes to his parents: 'I am in love with a hundred and one different things, fantasies and people, and finding no fixed point anywhere except in my pictures, at least one of which will, before the year is out, become as joyous and illuminating as almost anything one could imagine, unless one starts to use rockets to paint with' (late February). And a

The doll, 1919

Villa Romana, 29 Liebhartstalstrasse, *c.*1920
(Bohuslav Kokoschka in the foreground)

little later: 'Since Vienna I've been in love about 19 times . . . with heaps of serious, uniquely romantic ladies, in Frankfurt, Berlin and here . . . this means that I get a regular supply of love letters which act on me like the sun when it refuses to shine, and so they help me to paint wonderfully glowing colours'.

In spring, in the circle of the Dresden art collector Ida Bienert, meets the Russian Jewess Anna Kallin, who is studying singing in Dresden. For the next few years (until 1925) she is his closest friend and lover. Her figure appears in several paintings of the period, often together with that of another woman, Alice Graf-Lahmann, a friend of hers who also belongs to OK's circle.

4 June: Première of the opera *Murderer Hope of Women* by Hindemith in the *Landestheater*, Stuttgart; produced and designed by Oskar Schlemmer. Summer Exhibition of the *Dresdner Künstler-vereinigung* (Dresden Artists' Association), June–September; OK designs the poster, and is represented by twenty-five pictures.

November: Wolfgang Gurlitt in Berlin pub-lishes the lithographic cycle *Columbus in Chains* in book form.

Christmas in Vienna.

1922
January/February: owing to his father's illness, stays in Vienna till late February.

March: returns to Dresden; completes the picture 'Lot and his Daughters' which depicts OK with Anna Kallin and Alice Graf-Lahmann.

11 April: Travels to Venice with Dr Hans Posse to prepare his exhibition at the Biennale. Stays at the Hotel Bauer-Grünwald. In the German Pavilion allotted an exhibition room to himself, giving him equal status with Liebermann, Slevogt and Corinth. Has the walls painted black, so that the colours stand out more vividly. Twelve pictures shown from the Vienna and Dresden periods. Karl Scheffler writes a critique in *Kunst und Künstler*. The incessant rain in Venice stops him painting, so he makes a three-day excursion to Florence, where for the first time gazes in fascination at the works of Michelangelo. To his parents: 'In Florence Michelangelo's buildings, sculpture and paintings absolutely shattered me. Out in the street, for instance, you see an enormous marble statue, a naked David, just standing there, and it still makes an overwhelming impact on you, even though the figure has been standing there for a good 500 years. Almost every piece of work I saw moved me to tears, so majestic, so prodigious and magnificent was this genius's output' (May).

May: returns to Dresden. Intensive work on five pictures, presumably including two more Elbe landscapes. Writes to his father: 'I believe in all seriousness that now I really am the best painter on earth' (early summer).

Summer: works on the painting 'Rachel, Jacob and Leah', later called 'The Fountain'. 'I paint, paint and paint. I think it's been raining for 7 weeks now, but I haven't even noticed because I've never left the studio before 8 o'clock' (to his parents, 7 August). Produces several portrait lithographs.

December: persuades the Ministry for Internal Affairs in Dresden to extend Anna Kallin's residence permit by threatening to leave Dresden himself if 'his fiancée is not allowed to continue her studies'.

Undertakes his first opera production: designs the set for Hindemith's *Murderer Hope of Women*. In his print gallery Hugo Erfurth exhibits OK's entire graphic oeuvre. Inflation is reaching crisis point, and OK wants to leave Germany: '. . . I'm going to clear out of here in the spring. I can't stand this Germany any longer . . . Then I'll spend three months travelling about where it's really hot' (24 December).

1923
Spring: feels oppressed by his regimented life in Dresden; makes plans with Anna Kallin to move to Paris, or travel to Africa: 'I hate every picture I paint, I hate everything I am doing, I hate Europe, it's all just a shadow existence, and totally mean-ingless . . . Do you know what a real existence would be, Mirli? Africa! . . . I'd like to be a negro king and I'd drive out all the European moneybags and commercial travellers, and rouse the negroes to action. That would be a worthwhile and exciting enough task to make me want to go on living; and I'd like to confine those repulsive bourgeois solely to the continent of Europe, where they would have to exchange feathers, stamps and *Kitsch* pictures with each other until they are carried off to the cemetery . . .' (to Kallin, late March).

Works on the painting 'Jacob, Rachel and Leah'. 1–3 April in Berlin, to organize an exhi-bition of paintings and drawings at Cassirer's (March); stays at the Hotel Esplanade. From 5 April in Vienna, on account of his father's illness. Returns to Dresden presumably in late April and here works on 'Dresden, the Elbe Bridges (with figure from behind)' and 'Self-portrait with Crossed Arms'. Until summer works very hard to pay off loan for the Vienna house and to have enough pictures ready for an exhibition planned for America in the winter (which does not materialize).

June/July: from 21 June in Berlin, where he produces lithograph portraits of Liebermann, Gurlitt, the Berlin art dealer Victor Wallerstein and others. Takes part in the debate about Europe's dependence on mineral oil, and gives a lecture on the existence of organic oil in the Vienna Basin (the residue of sea creatures).

August: travels to Switzerland with Anna Kallin, visiting Zurich (25 August) Lucerne, Les Avants, Montreux (31 August) and Blonay (5 September–early October). From the terrace of the former Hôtel de Blonay paints 'Lac Léman I'. The Saxon Ministry for Internal Affairs questions Cassirer's about OK's whereabouts, and is told he has already left Germany and is residing abroad (30 August).

8 September: requests the Ministry for Internal Affairs in Dresden to give him a two-year sabbatical for travel abroad, which is granted on 24 September.

26 September: for the *Berliner Tagblatt* he writes the article 'Persian Letter', in which he gives his views on the ending of the strike in the Ruhr during the French occupation and on Europe's dependence on oil (unpublished).

5 October: stays at Zurich for a group exhibition at the Wolfsberg Art Salon which includes some of his watercolours and drawings. Subsequently in Vienna, where on 23 October his father dies. Stays till the end of the year with his family at 29, Liebhartstalstrasse.

The composer Ernst Krěnek sets *Orpheus and Eurydice* to music.

Kokoschka's father, Dresden, 1918

1924

March: in Vienna, starts work on the portrait of Schoenberg. In Berlin the Goldschmidt-Wallerstein Gallery exhibits paintings, lithographs and watercolours. The Goltz Gallery in Munich exhibits graphic works. On 16 March in the *Münchner Allgemeine Zeitung*, Wilhelm Hausenstein writes an enthusiastic article about OK.

April/May: travels to Venice, where he paints 'Venice, Boats at the Dogana' from the balcony of the Hotel Danieli, 'from two different windows, two different angles of vision, so that I doubled the width of my visual field, an experiment I have often repeated since' (*My Life*). Travels on to Florence. From the Excelsior Hotel paints the view over the Arno ('Florence, Banks of the Arno'). Late May, returns to Vienna, where the Neue Galerie shows about 100 of his watercolours and graphic works (June/July). Paints 'The Artist and his Model II'.

13 October: The Neue Galerie in Vienna opens a one-man show with seventeen early paintings. Together with the summer exhibition in the same gallery this is the first show of his work in Vienna for thirteen years. Two weeks later it has to be closed because a painting is slashed by a visitor. OK writes a bitter letter, published in several newspapers: 'This incident is, as far as my personal experience allows me to judge, symptomatic of the sterility and criminal exhibitionism of this whole society, which is nurtured by a press without any understanding of creative activity. It was this same press which reviled my paintings in the *Kunstschau* of 1907 [*sic*] . . . and which denounced me while I tried to teach art here to children, apprentices and students.'

21 October: with Loos and the painter Sebastian Isepp to Paris. They stay on the Ile Saint-Louis, at 20 Quai d'Orleans, in the house owned by Jan Slivinsky, ex-director of the Vienna Imperial Library.

7 November: moves to the Hôtel Foyot, in the Rue Tournon. Is not at home in Paris, and writes to Vienna: 'It is cold and wet, and everything about Paris is wrong for me . . . I'm bored and will find it very difficult to start any work . . . unless you stay at the Ritz or Claridge's Hotel, you notice at first hand how much hardship there is here; and I am left with a feeling of deep depression and helplessness, where others expect to find sensation and orgiastic pleasure. I am extremely unhappy, and even a little repelled by life' (to Lotte Mandel, early November). Avoids artists' rendezvous e.g. Café du Dôme and Deux Magots, since has no time for the *Geniemarkt* (genius market). Becomes friendly with the deaf and dumb Hungarian painter, Tihany. Helps out a tubercular prostitute, and arranges for her to go into hospital, where she dies on 8 November. Paints Nancy

Cunard's portrait (from 18 November) and a little later the view of the Paris Opera ('Paris, The Opera'; 'Paris, The Roof of the Opera') from the Grand Hôtel.

December: from 19 December in Zurich, where he tries to arrange an exhibition. End of the year, returns to Vienna.

The Hamburg Kunsthalle acquires the picture of Florence and purchases 'The Tempest' for 13,500 marks.

1925

January: travels from Vienna to Dresden to prepare for a comprehensive retrospective of his works at the Arnold Gallery, consisting of forty-eight oils and almost his entire graphic oeuvre (18 January–late February). In *Der Cicerone* Will Grohmann comments: 'If the early works are overshadowed by the magic of psychological analysis, the late works are dominated by the will of a prophet who would like to paint murals for new temples, which even in a poorly-lit space are intensely vivid'.

Subsequently in Berlin, where he makes plans for extended trips around Europe. Paul Cassirer grants him unlimited credit for this, set off against future sales of pictures.

7 February: short stay in Vienna, where he completes his second portrait of Karl Kraus. 17/18 February: travels via Geneva to Monte Carlo, accompanied by the Frankfurt banker and art-dealer Jakob Goldschmidt. Goldschmidt makes all the travel arrangements and organizes the dispatch of the completed pictures. From the Grand Hotel OK paints his first travel picture, the view of the Bay of Monte Carlo (completed 24 February).

March: 25 February–3 March in Nice (Hôtel Royal). Paints a still-life of roses. 4–8 March: in Marseilles (Hôtel de Noailles). On his first day (5 March) paints the view towards the harbour, and immediately afterwards a second harbour picture (completed 7 March, 'Marseilles Harbour I and II'). 9–11 March: at Avignon (Hôtel Dominion), paints 'Avignon'; writes to his brother: 'Up to now everything has been soulless *Kitsch* – Nice, Monte Carlo. But now I am experiencing reality . . . here I find history and life' (9 March). 10 March: at Remoulins; 12 and 13 March: at Montpellier (Hôtel Metropole); 14–16 March: at Aigues-Mortes. Here, from the Porte des Remblais, on the city wall paints the picture 'Aigues-Mortes'. Takes an active interest in the history of the Catharist sect. In Les-Saint-Maries-de-la-Mer joins in the celebration organized by gypsies from all over the world in honour of the Black Madonna (short story 'Aigues-Mortes'). 19–23 March: stays at Vernet-les-Bains (Hôtel du Portugal) in the Pyrenees, waits

for a visa for Spain and paints a view of the town. 22 March at Montelimar, 28 March Toulouse (Hôtel Compagnie du Midi).

April: 29 March–3 April: stays at Bordeaux; from the street, paints the western part of Notre-Dame (completed on 31 March) and from the Grand Hôtel paints the view towards the Place de la Bourse with the Grand Théâtre. 8–13 April: Biarritz. Romance with Marguerite Loeb, a young American student. Paints 'Biarritz Beach' and 'Biarritz Rocks'. 14 April: by train to Lisbon (15–19 April); begins to paint the view across the harbour from the fortress of Lisbon, but the military coup and the resulting turmoil prevent him from continuing. Instead, paints 'Street Scene, Lisbon'. From 23 April in Madrid. From a window in the Palace Hotel paints the picture 'Madrid, Plaza Cánovas del Castillo'. Frequent visits to the Prado and the Escorial where he is deeply impressed by the paintings of Velasquez. Writes to his sister: 'Velasquez – what divine painting! I can't paint any more, tell mother, because in his presence I am completely overawed' (25 April). Sees his first bull-fight and considers it a cowardly, nauseating spectacle. By late April has visited Seville, Toledo (28 April) and Aranjuez (30 April).

11 May: returns to Paris, where he stays for three months. Sells all the travel pictures so far completed to Cassirer and Goldschmidt, so that – as he reports home – from 1 December he is able to deposit a total of 70,000 marks in a Swiss bank: 'the first money I've ever saved in my life' (11 May). In the Savoy Hotel rents a 'disgracefully expensive' apartment, and takes lessons in English and French conversation. Paints the Louvre and two pictures of the Tuileries.

Summer: in mid-June has to go into hospital because of a broken nose. At the Kunsthaus Zurich is represented at the *International Exhibition* by ten pictures.

Early July: travels to Holland, again accompanied by Goldschmidt, 'with the idea of spending six months painting and being dragged around to as many places as possible!' (2 July, to Anna Kallin). 5–8 July: in Scheveningen (Kurhaushotel), where he paints two flower still-lifes and writes home: 'Holland is the most beautiful country I've seen so far' (7 July). 9 July: Continues his journey via The Hague to London. Stays ten days, living at the Abbotsford Hotel, 4 Upper Montague Street. Paints 'Tower Bridge'.

August: 25 July–5 August: stays at Amsterdam (Doelenhotel) and paints four pictures: two views from his hotel window, one of the canals and one of the Nieuwe Markt. Again meets Marguerite Loeb, with whom he has kept up a charming correspondence since their romance in Biarritz. Subsequently, travels to the Engadine, to Pontresina (Hotel Kronenhof Bellavista), where he stays until late August.

Autumn: presumably in September returns to Vienna. 13 October: the Dresden Academy asks whether he wishes to resume his teaching duties, since his two-year sabbatical is now over. OK does not want to resign, and requests a further year's leave of absence, which the Academy grants.

The 24th International Exhibition at the Carnegie Institute, Pittsburgh, USA (15 October–16 December) includes two pictures by OK.

November: in Berlin, Cassirer exhibits all thirty-five travel pictures; and, as Julius Meier-Graefe reports in the *Frankfurter Zeitung* 'an enthusiastic crowd mills around in front of the pictures', the 'huge success of these landscapes is confirmed . . . by the comparatively high prices they fetch'.

Libretto and score of the opera *Orpheus and Eurydice* by Ernst Krěnek published. The Cassirer Verlag issues a second, expanded monograph on the artist by Paul Westheim. Many newspapers and periodicals print reviews of his works.

1926

7 January: Paul Cassirer commits suicide; OK goes to Berlin for a discussion with his successors Grete Ring and Walter Feilchenfeldt. From Berlin writes to his mother: 'Everything here has been sorted out, and we've agreed that I'll make another longish trip this year, perhaps to Egypt or somewhere similar, to paint landscapes' (27 January). From the window of his room in the Adlon Hotel paints the 'Brandenburg Gate'. In his Frankfurt gallery Goldschmidt exhibits the 1925 travel pictures.

14–17 February: visits Hamburg and Lübeck. From the Hotel Vier Jahreszeiten in Hamburg paints a view of the Alster. Subsequently back in Berlin again, where he stays in the home 'of the old tiger Paul Cassirer' (to his mother, February).

Spring/Summer: in mid-March, accompanied by Guttmann from the Cassirer Gallery makes his second trip to London, and stays almost six months. At Dover paints the view of the sea and cliffs. Lives first at the Savoy Hotel (10 March–28 April), and from May onwards at 12, Ovington Gardens, off Brompton Road. From the 8th floor of the Savoy paints two views of the Thames, one upstream, the other downstream. Paints a portrait of the dancer Adèle Astaire. Is given permission to work in the Zoo before normal visiting hours, enabling him to paint 'Tigon' and 'Mandrill'.

June/September: at the *International Art Exhibition* in Dresden represented by seven fairly recent oils.

Autumn: 30 September: stays in Paris, late October back in Vienna.

November: travels to Berlin via Dresden (10 November). In Dresden negotiates another extension of leave of absence from the Academy. In Berlin starts the portrait of Leo Kestenberg, a pupil of Busoni who is in charge of musical education in Prussia.

27 November: in Kassel, for the première of Krěnek's opera *Orpheus and Eurydice*.

The Moritzburg State Gallery in Halle purchases 'The Exiles' for 13,500 marks, and the Städel in Frankfurt acquires the painting of 'Monte Carlo' for 6,000 marks.

Some of OK's letters to the doll-maker, Hermine Moos, are published by Paul Westheim.

In Volume 16 of the Propyläen History of Art *The Art of the 20th Century* Carl Einstein writes an essay on OK.

1927

Spring: early January, in Vienna, from 11 January back in Berlin, where he stays till mid-May, again at Cassirer's house. On 12 January in the Aquarium of Berlin Zoo, begins the picture 'Giant Turtles'.

The Flechtheim Gallery exhibits Nell Walden's art collection, which contains works by OK, including the portrait of Herwarth Walden. In February Cassirer's holds the exhibition *Portraits by Oskar Kokoschka: People and Animals*. Meier-Graefe reviews it in the *Frankfurter Zeitung* (2 February).

June: from 5 June, the Kunsthaus, Zurich holds the largest exhibition of his work to date, consisting of 101 paintings, forty-nine watercolours and drawings, as well as 110 prints (6 June–3 July). It is evident from the catalogue that all the leading museums in Germany have purchased works by OK. Siegfried Giedion writes an article on him in *Der Cicerone*. OK attends the exhibition in early July. 16 June: the professorial council of the Dresden Academy resolves to replace him as professor 'since it appears impossible to secure a permanent assent from Kokoschka'. His successor is Otto Dix.

Autumn: late September, travels to Venice (Europa-Britannia Hotel, now the Bristol Hotel). From a hotel window paints the view towards Santa Maria della Salute ('Venice, Santa Maria della Salute I'). 1 October: Dr Lütjens, from Cassirer's in Amsterdam, comes to Venice to accompany him. 7 October: visits Giotto's Capella degli Scrovegni at Padua. 8–12 October: in Turin. Travels on to Switzerland, visiting Courmayeur (15–22 October). On 16 October begins to paint the view of 'Les Dents des Géants' (completed 22 October). Reports to his mother: 'I'm firmly stuck in the ice, every day I climb 1,000–1,200 metres over it, and

paint pictures with my fingers frozen' (19 October). Subsequently at Chamonix (23 October–6 November). Each day goes up the mountains on the cable-railway, and paints Mont Blanc ('Chamonix-Mont Blanc', 28 October–9 November). Writes to his family: 'I'm already on my fourth picture, and I haven't felt so fresh for years. Every morning, despite the freezing cold, I do some climbing in the mountains from about 7.30 or 8.00 until 12 noon, never less than 800–1,000 metres up . . . and then paint till 4.30 . . . That Mont Blanc is a sorcerer' (31 October).

November/December: 10–18 November: stays at Annécy (Hôtel des Négociants). Lütjens has gone to Amsterdam and OK feels uncomfortable on his own. Paints 'Lac d'Annécy I', and writes home: 'There's snow here and it's miserably boring. I'm painting in a house 1½ hours away from the site, with the window open, and at 4 o'clock the world stops dead' (13 November).

Travels on alone to Lyons (18 November–8 December, Hôtel Royal). Writes to Anna Kallin: 'There's nothing but rain and fog here, and I'm waiting for Lütjens to travel on with me into the Loire district' (23 November). After Lütjens's return (23 November) paints the picture 'Lyons' from a house in the Jardin des Chatreux situated on rising ground above the Saône. Travels via Tour (11 December) and Blois to Paris, where he stays at the Hôtel Lutétia, remaining there till January 1928. Makes preparations for a trip to Africa with Lütjens. In Holland Lütjens organizes a touring exhibition of OK's travel pictures, which goes to Amsterdam, Rotterdam and The Hague. In the *Thieme-Becker Lexicon of Artists* Hans Tietze writes an entry on OK.

1928

2 January: in Marseilles embarks for Africa with Lütjens. 4 January: reaches Carthage, 5 January: arrives at Tunis (Hôtel Atlantique). From the roof of a greengrocer's shop starts to paint 'Market Place in Tunis'. Reports to Anna Kallin: 'From 1–6 I paint, by the evening I'm tired, so go to bed at 9, then in the mornings from 9–12 I have 'flu, so stay in bed' (8 January).

For the next two weeks it rains incessantly, the greengrocer's roof collapses and OK has to stop painting. Excursions to Carthage, on 19 January travels on via Sfax to Tozeur (Hôtel Transatlantique), and stays there till early February. On 22 January in Tozeur begins a painting standing on the minaret of a mosque, which he fails to complete 'because it's too windy and boring up there' (to his family, 27 January).

Forms a friendship with a sheikh from a Bedouin

tribe, who allows him to paint two women in his family. From 27–29 January, in the desert, paints the picture 'Arab Women', and writes about it to Anna Kallin: 'I have to admit, I flirted with two Bedouin women for two whole days, and in the process managed to complete my first painting. Tomorrow, the caravan moves off again. A sparkling picture. How to flirt in Arabic' (29 January).

February: travels on to Algeria, stays from 9 January to 29 January in Biskra (Hôtel Transatlantique) and its environs; in the north of the city paints the oasis 'El Kantara' (12–18 February), writes to Anna Kallin: 'Here, for the first time on this entire trip, on a walk over the sand dunes I felt the most profound sense of peace and real happiness. In the afternoons I always paint' (16 February), and a little later: 'my painting isn't bad . . . [I'm] now beginning to paint really well. And from now on I'll paint more, because by now I know the country better. Everything is infinitely vast and without tangible form' (18 February, to his mother). From 23 February to 29 February he is driven by car every morning to the Col de Sfa, to the north of Biskra, and here paints 'Exodus, Col de Sfa'.

3–20 March: stays at Touggourt. Given permission to paint a portrait of Sidi Ahmet Ben Tidjani, the Marabout of Temacine, regarded as a holy man. By the end of Ramadan the painting is finished, and he is invited to a sumptuous feast in the palace; as a special delicacy served the eye of a roasted sheep. From 23 March stays in Algiers, whilst Lütjens returns to Europe.

4 April: travels back via Morocco and Gibraltar to Seville (9 April). From 18 April–1 May: stays in Madrid (Palace Hotel). Feels uncomfortable on his own and writes to Anna Kallin: 'I am so confused and apathetic that since Touggourt I haven't done anything else at all' (21 April); and slightly later: '. . . but you must realise that people like me, who know the Promised Land with all their soul will never actually reach it. In Madrid I saw such a wonderfully melancholy and noble picture of Adam and Eve by Titian that I spent whole days gazing at it . . . and almost forgot that I hadn't painted it' (4 May). Excursions to Toledo and Aranjuez.

The Berlin National Gallery's exhibition *Recent German Art from Private Collections in Berlin*, includes several pictures by OK.

4 May: stays in Barcelona (Ritz Hotel). Subsequently, travels to Switzerland and Garmisch-Partenkirchen (Bavaria), where presumably paints the portrait of the Hungarian collector Marczell von Nemeš.

Summer: In early June stays in London (Burlington Hotel). An exhibition at the Leicester Galleries shows thirty-four of his pictures, the first presentation of his work in Britain; the English public shows little interest and the press reacts unfavourably ('a mass of tricks of hand' – Walter Bayes in *The Saturday Review*, 23 June). Travels to Ireland, again accompanied by Lütjens. From Dublin they go on to Killarney (24 June–1 July). Lütjens then goes home, but OK wanders up and down the coast by way of Valentia (3 July) and Dingia to Galway. From 5 July–16 July back in Dublin (Gresham Hotel). Subsequently goes on to visit Raitnige (20 July) and the island of Achill on the north-west coast (21–late July), where as he writes to Anna Kallin he 'would so love to paint Titian women (and get to know them) – for they certainly are there. They ride horses and donkeys bareback' (20 July).

August: Short visit to Oxford; admires the antiquities in the Ashmolean. Returns to Vienna.

In November again in London, in December returns to Vienna via Paris.

1929
Spring: with Albert Ehrenstein goes on a cruise to Egypt and Palestine. Embarks 24 February at Brindisi. From late February to early April they stay at Alexandria (27 February) and Cairo (from 4 March, Bristol Hotel). OK paints the 'Pyramids of Gizeh' (4–11 March). 14 March: is introduced to Princess Eloui, widow of the assassinated heir to the Moroccan throne and, according to OK, 'the most beautiful woman I have yet seen in my life, a Turkoman. Perhaps I shall be allowed to paint her' (to his family, 14 March). But the plan fails to materialize because 'I couldn't offer her an oasis at the moment when she wanted to be alone with me or because I couldn't have a Rolls Royce waiting outside her door in which to elope with her . . .' (to Marcel von Nemeš, 25 May). Paints 'Arab Women and Child' (20–21 March).

April: to Palestine, stopping first in Jerusalem (13–21 April, Fast Palestina Hotel), where on 14 April begins to paint the view over the city from a Jewish cemetery situated outside it. Subsequently travels by bus through the desert to the Dead Sea, and Jericho, where he visits the archaeological site (short story 'Jericho'). Goes on to Tel Aviv (23–26 April), Damascus and Beirut (13–18 May, Hôtel d'Orient). Leaves Ehrenstein behind in Palestine

Kokoschka in North Africa, February 1928

Tomich Hotel, Strathglass, Inverness-shire

and on 24 May travels on to Greece. From Athens writes to his brother: '. . . visited the Acropolis and a museum . . . Miracle upon miracle . . . It puts everything I have so far known in the shade . . .'. Stays only a couple of days and on 27 May goes by ship to Istanbul (Pera Palace Hotel).

Summer: until mid-July in Istanbul. Paints the view across the Bosphorus towards the Old City ('Istanbul', completed late June.) Returns via Athens (19 July) and Venice (25 July) to Zurich (29 July); in Zurich again meets Damaris Brunow, a relative of Alice Lahmann's from Dresden, whom he has admired for some while.

August: travels to Morayshire in N.E. Scotland accompanied by Walter Feilchenfeldt of Cassirer's. 15 August: at Glenernie, Dunphail with friends of Feilchenfeldt (the brothers Kurt and Rudolph Hahn), from where OK writes home: 'Here's a country house full of delightful people, a mountain torrent like in our Alps, pretty far north, near the sea'. Subsequently to Nairn, then (from 23 August) stays for about a week with a farmer's family at Dulsie Bridge on the Findhorn River (short story 'Ann Eliza Reed'). Paints 'Dulsie Bridge' and 'Junction of the Divie and Findhorn Rivers'. From 2 September to 5 September stays at Inverness (Royal Hotel) and writes home: 'The rain here is pitiless, and there's also thick mist. Today I'm going to a small guest-house by a torrential river in the Highlands . . .' (5 September). Stays until at least 21 September at the Tomich Hotel, Strathglass, Inverness-shire, where he paints the 'Plodda Falls'. Presumably stays briefly in Edinburgh before going back to the Continent. On 4 October in Rouen, and later in Paris (Hôtel Vouillemont, Rue Boissy d'Anglas). Passes the winter in Paris.

Georg Biermann and Hans Heilmair each publish a short monograph on OK; an article about him appears in the *Encyclopaedia Britannica*.

1930

January: elected a member of the Prussian Academy of Arts (Berlin).

Spring: March: travels to North Africa with Lütjens, visiting Tunis (Hôtel Transatlantique 8–11 March), Sfax (15 March) and then via Gabes to the ferry for the island of Djerba.

April: stays from 24 March to 11 April in Houmt Souk (Grand Hotel) on Djerba. Hires a chauffeur and is driven around the island. In the Jewish quarter of Houmt Souk wants to paint the municipal chief's beautiful daughter. After the first sitting is broken off, makes a risky attempt, aided and abetted by an old witchdoctor in Hara Kebira, to see the girl again and abduct her. Describes the episode to Anna Kallin: 'The whole country –

from north to south – from here as far as Tunis, is up in arms about me, the French Général Résident, the Contrôleur Civil of the island, the Jewish Sheikh of the village, the girl's fiancé . . .' (22 June). But his plan comes to nothing. Paints 'Fishes on the Beach of Djerba'. Returns by way of Tripoli (17 April) to Tunis (18 April). Spends a week in Kairouan (24 April–2 May), and subsequently back in Tunis (2 May–17 May). Travels back via Italy.

Summer: in Rome (from 23 May, Savoy Hotel) and Anticoli, a village in the Sabine Hills (22 July–early August). Paints 'Anticoli, Harvest in the Sabine Hills' (completed 6 August). Travels on to France, visiting Annécy (31 August), where he again meets Damaris Brunow. Paints a second view of the 'Lac d'Annécy' and begins the portrait of Damaris ('Swedish Woman'), with a self-portrait in the background. Subsequently stays in Vannes Morbihan in Brittany (13 September).

Autumn: first onslaughts from the National Socialists. Under orders from the Nazi Minister, Frick, OK's pictures in the Castle Museum in Weimar are impounded. In his book *Art and Race* Paul Schultze-Naumburg compares a portrait by OK with paintings by mental patients.

From 21 September in Paris (Hôtel Vouillemont) where he stays a year. Occupies a studio at 9, Rue Delambre, above Augustus John. Thanks to John is introduced to James Joyce. As OK later recalls, John was 'a giant in physique, but he could not hold his liquor, and I often used to have to hold his head over the gutter in the grey light of morning' (*My Life*).

1931

January: the Kunsthalle Mannheim holds a major retrospective of his works (18 January–1 March), with catalogue containing contributions from friends and acquaintances, including Adolf Loos, Carl Moll, Eugenie Schwarzwald and Walter Hasenclever. In the catalogue Max Liebermann writes: 'Among artists now in middle life, Kokoschka is undoubtedly one of the most gifted . . . Kokoschka is a born painter'.

February: first exhibition in Paris at the Bonjean Gallery (*German Painters*, with six pictures by OK). Favourable notices in France (*Beaux Arts*) and America. 'All the interest of the German showing . . . is concentrated on the half dozen canvases by Kokoschka. These are powerful representations with the stormy depths of Tintoretto, of El Greco, producing a strong impression of tragedy.' (*Art News*). In the major exhibition *German Painting and Sculpture* at the Museum of Modern Art, New York, represented by four pictures (March–April).

From 18 March the Galeries Georges Petit, Paris

holds a one-man show which makes a big impact in France. The *Frankfurter Zeitung* writes: 'Its success with the public is certainly considerable, the vernissage was . . . attended by a large number of genuinely interested people . . . It is also worth mentioning that even now, over two weeks later, interest has not waned, and that one . . . still finds a constant stream of pensive and attentive viewers' (5 April). The first critique in Italy appears in the periodical *L'Arte*.

April: Owing to the difficult economic situation and a more limited sales potential for pictures, Cassirer's wants to reduce the artist's monthly income to a fixed sum of 2,000 marks. OK refuses, and dissolves his contract with the gallery.

June: after the suicide of the painter Jules Pascin OK moves into his house, the Villa des Camélias in Auteuil (Paris XIV). Describes his new home in a letter to A. Rosenlew: 'My bed is a *lit de camp*, so short, so narrow, so cold and hard that I wake up every hour . . . I have one yellow, one green, and one blue room, as well as a large bathroom . . . with an enormous studio above, which has an enormous mirror in it. But apart from a drawing-table and my camp-bed and a few straw stools, not a stick of furniture. A delightful maid and lots of cognac and a tiny garden no bigger than a bath' (11 June).

Exhibition *Vom Abbild zum Sinnbild* (From Illustration to Symbol) at the Städel, Frankfurt includes seven pictures by OK.

September: Without a regular contract and in the wake of the economic crisis of 1929, again in financial straits. Stays in Vienna with his family from 5 September 1931–March 1932. Com-

Vienna, late 1931, with 'Double portrait of Trudl'

missioned by the Viennese City Authorities, paints the picture 'Vienna, View from the Wilhelminenberg'.

Begins the series of 'Trudl' pictures of a young girl living nearby in the Liebhartstal.

November: visited at the Liebhartstal house by Meier-Graefe, who praises his recent paintings in the *Frankfurter Zeitung*, and observes: 'He needs public acclaim more than anything. All the art critics except those in Vienna declare that he is the greatest, the most subtle, the most ingenious of painters. Even in Paris an untold number of critics have written in these terms. The only exception is Vienna. Oskar Kokoschka is basking in Vienna's neglect.' OK stays in Vienna until spring 1932.

1932

February: the Rudolf Probst Gallery, Dresden exhibits a number of his oils and drawings. Probst helps financially by selling some pictures.

5 March: back in Paris, at the Villa des Camélias. Works on 'The Fountain' (begun in Dresden in 1922). Makes contact with the Bernheim Jeune Gallery, where he puts some of his pictures on sale. Makes strenuous efforts to establish contact with American art dealers. Writes to Probst: 'I'm having a tremendously difficult time because legally I can't get any money out of Austria and because I never see a soul here, and am stuck in my studio all day working like a maniac . . .' (24 April). Presumably paints 'Self-portrait with Cap'.

Summer: in the Austrian Pavilion at the Venice Biennale represented by a number of oils and drawings. In Paris gets a telegram of congratulation from Max Liebermann, which he finds very encouraging.

October: together with Duhamel and Romain Rolland, elected a member of the 'Rendezvous-Internationale' Committee, which strives to promote cultural exchanges. Under its auspices, OK would like to organize a Max Liebermann exhibition in Paris, 'as a gesture of cultural homage and reconciliation vis-à-vis Germany' (to H. Simon, 15 October).

A catalogue of his drawings is printed, with a preface by Paul Westheim (the book does not appear until 1935).

1933

Stays in Paris until May. On 30 January Hitler becomes Reich Chancellor; the *Deutsche Kultur-Korrespondenz* (German Cultural Correspondence) demands the removal of 'all products with cosmopolitan or Bolshevist association' from German museums.

May: as a result of the 'Aryan Paragraph'

Liebermann, as a Jew, is forced to resign from the Prussian Academy of Arts. OK writes the article 'The Voice Which Max Liebermann Lacked' published 8 June in the *Frankfurter Zeitung*. Five pictures by the artist in the Dresden art collections are impounded. OK leaves Paris, and from 10 May to late August stays at Rapallo (Albergo Ristorante Rosa Bianca).

Summer: in Rapallo paints the Consul Bob Gesinus Visser and his wife. His stay at Visser's house ends unpleasantly as he reports to his friend Ehrenstein: 'Here I fell into the clutches of a real gigolo, who paid my debts for me in Paris and then wanted to turn me into a real factory, until I was forced to hit him' (June). Paints several landscapes in the area around Rapallo ('Santa Margherita, Boats', 'Ligurian Landscape', 'Rapallo, View of the Bay') and writes the story of his childhood, which is published in November under the title 'From the Biography of My Youth' (in *Der Wiener Kunstwanderer*).

Late August: stays in Zurich, and presumably also in Genoa, where he paints the picture, 'Genoa, View of the Harbour'.

Autumn: 23 August: Death of Adolf Loos at Kalksburg, near Vienna. OK moves into his mother's house in the Liebhartstal; gives a memorial address for Loos to the Wiener Werkbund.

1 November: Thomas Mann writes of OK: 'For a long time, in fact, I have regarded Kokoschka as the quintessence of modern painting. I love, understand, and admire the art of painting in our age first and foremost in his work . . . civilized magic – that is what it seems to me Kokoschka's pictures embody . . . he is a skilful dreamer, a master of precise fantasy, in whose magical work spirit becomes nature and reality visibly conveys the spiritual' (in *Der Wiener Kunstwanderer*, November).

Winter: in December the Hugo Feigl Gallery in Prague shows fourteen recent oils.

At the end of the year writes the political essay 'Totem and Taboo, Intellectual Exercises of a Cynic', in which he takes issue with the Nazis' false cultural myths, and pleads for a more positive form of national education.

1934

Spring: concerned about the political situation in Germany and Austria. From 15 January to 6 February stays in Budapest. On 18 January gives the speech 'On the *Via Lucis* of Comenius' in which he discusses the need to educate the German nation into being politically responsible citizens.

February: shortly after his return to Vienna, civil war breaks out (the *Starhembergputsch*, 12–15 February). OK deeply distressed by the bombard-

ment of working-class quarters by government troops.

March: would like to leave Vienna, 'because for three months I haven't painted anything at all . . . But I'll only be able to start painting again once I've earned some money and have got away from here. The city doesn't interest me any more and there are no portrait commissions . . .' (to Hilde Goldschmidt, 11 March). Through Hugo Feigl in Prague given permission to paint the portrait of the President of the Czechoslovakian Republic, Thomas G. Masaryk.

April: the proscription of all political parties except the Fatherland Front led by the Chancellor, Dollfuss, marks the end of democratic government in Austria. In his essay 'Thomas Paine or the Social State' OK condemns the authoritarian constitution of the Dollfuss regime.

Summer: mother's illness and death (4 July). Her body is transported to Hollenstein. OK and his brother have a small chapel erected in her memory at the Bergfriedhof (cemetery), for which they need to borrow a great deal of money. Makes plans with Ehrenstein for a long journey to Russia and China: 'If I get into a train again it must be one going all the way to China; I intend to drown myself in a junk loaded with whisky. Since my mother's death life has lost a lot of its appeal for me . . .' (to Ehrenstein, August/September).

Autumn: in September writes the autobiographical short story 'The Wounding'. On 25 September goes to Prague (Ambassador Hotel), where initially plans to stay for ten days, to paint and

Kokoschka, Vienna, 1933

earn enough money for his projected journey to Russia. His sister Berta has been living in Prague since 1918 (Strašnice, Prague XX, 50 Na Třebešině). On 5 October writes to Anna Kallin: 'After a very long year I'm away from Vienna again and don't yet know where I'm going next . . . Since Paris I haven't done any work at all but had to borrow a lot of money. In Vienna I was almost driven into politics by those princely gigolos, liberal cannon-crusaders and Catholic bully-boys who, in order to boost the tourist trade . . . put the entire rural population of Austria into concentration camps . . . But instead of spies . . . Gauleiters and Almighty God as the first words of the constitution they ought to introduce matriarchy and workers' rights into the *Volksschule*' (5 October).

Autumn/Winter: in the Prämonstratenser Monastery on the Strahov paints his first view of Prague. By the end of the year has produced three more cityscapes. Becomes friendly with Hugo Feigl, 'who spent days wandering around the city with me, to find viewpoints from which to paint. He persuaded the owners of flats, gardens and houses which I thought would offer me good vantage-points, to let me paint there, and in the end also managed to get collectors to buy the resulting pictures' (*My Life*). Drops the idea of going to Russia and decides to stay in Prague. As he later recalls: 'I liked being in Prague. The city had once more become a cosmopolitan centre, as it had been after the Thirty Years War. Here, for the last time, all Europe could meet' (*My Life*). At Dr. K.B. Palkovsky's house he meets Olda Palkovská, his future wife. Moves into the Juliš Hotel on Wenceslaus Square (now the Tatjan Hotel).

1935

Dictatorship in Germany and an increasingly threatening political situation in Europe impel OK to speak out, in essays and lectures, for humanistic ideas. Produces two more Prague cityscapes.

Spring: 8 February: Max Liebermann dies in Berlin. On 20 February in the Prague periodical *The Truth* an article by OK appears with the title: 'Living and Dead Art. A Conversation with Max Liebermann'.

In April the Kunsthaus, Zurich exhibits twenty-five of his travel pictures. The Modern Gallery in Prague buys the painting 'Prague, Charles Bridge'.

Summer: from 10 June on his country estate at Lány, begins the portrait of the Czech President, Thomas G. Masaryk, whom he regards as the incarnation of a pugnacious humanist. In conversations with Masaryk OK deepens his knowledge of the ideas of the Moravian Bishop, J.A. Comenius.

In June: an aliens' law is passed by the Czech government, forbidding immigrants any form of political activity. Masaryk helps OK to obtain Czech citizenship. Occupies a studio in a tower at Bellevue House, near the Crusaders' Monastery. From his window looks out over the Moldau, with the Charles Bridge and the Hradschin above it. On 6 July in the *Prague Daily News* he writes the article 'Humanity Through *Volksschule*'.

Autumn: foundation of the Union for Justice and Freedom in Prague (26 September), a non-partisan organization of intellectuals, opposed to the destruction of culture and abuse of human rights. OK supports these efforts with essays and lectures. Writes three political articles: 'Two Kinds of Justice', 'Jeremy Bentham contra the Sovereign State', and 'What will the League of Nations learn from the Abyssinian Exploit?' (not published until 1975).

The volume of his drawings published by Ernst Rathenau is confiscated in Germany.

1936

March: as a member of the Czech delegation attends the Peace Conference in Brussels. On 7 March gives a lecture, extracts from which are published in the *Prague Daily News*.

Considers going to America, and asks the art dealer W.R. Valentiner to mediate for him: 'I was stupid not to have come to the States with you, for by now I would have been world-famous over there, whereas here in Europe the houses of cards collapse

Olda Palkovská on Kokoschka's studio balcony, Prague, 1935 or 1936

as soon as you build them . . . Could one paint the President of the United States?' (25 March)

Summer: 11 July: compromise treaty between Hitler and the Austrian Chancellor Kurt von Schuschnigg, whereby Austria is declared a 'German State'. The Prague journal *The Truth* prints OK's article 'Domine Quo Vadis', a warning against the 'cultural oblivion' and the 'ethical nadir' represented by Nazi ideology, which 'inevitably leads to the atrocities of mass-executions, the system of torture and hostages, the institutions of the Secret Police . . . and the greatest disgrace of the century, the concentration camps.' In essays and speeches addresses himself to the students of Prague. Begins work on the drama *Comenius*.

Autumn: in September, from his studio, paints a broader vista of Prague (presumably 'Prague, View from the Moldau Pier I'). Writes to Carl Moll: 'I've already started painting a large-scale work; I hope I'm lucky with the weather, so that it will be finished really soon. I'm making it purely picturesque, not topographic, and now there is a bluish-French air here by the river' (18 September).

In October his portrait of Masaryk is exhibited at the Carnegie Institute, Pittsburgh, U.S.A.

1937

February: gives lectures in the Bert Brecht Club, an association of emigré artists in Prague.

March: in his essay 'At the Eleventh Hour', which appears on 1 February and 22 February in *The Truth*, again points out the necessity of educational reform.

28 March: the Prague Artists' Association Manés elects him a corresponding member, along with Le Corbusier, Ernst, Gropius and Chagall, among others.

May: the Austrian Museum for Art and Industry opens the first major Kokoschka retrospective in Vienna, with thirty-eight paintings, sixty-four drawings and prints from all periods (May–June). OK refuses to attend.

Summer: 19 July: opening in Munich of the Nazi exhibition of *Degenerate 'Art'* (19 July–30 November). With a number of modifications, it is shown throughout Germany up until summer 1939. Eight paintings by OK are shown, including 'The Tempest' from Hamburg, 'The Exiles' from Halle, 'The Pagans' from Dresden, the portrait of the 'Duchess of Montesquiou' from Hagen, and 'Monte Carlo' from Frankfurt. In the exhibition guide two of OK's drawings are reproduced next to one by a mental patient. By the end of the year some 400 works by OK in German museums have been impounded.

In response, OK writes the essay 'Degenerate

Art' in which he says 'Europe trembles in fear before that hypnotist who – overnight it seems – has transplanted the sorcery of the ancient oriental priest-kings . . . right into the present-day world of spectacular technological progress and blatant materialism' (not published until 1975). In addition, he writes the article 'The Modern State – an Absurdity'.

Emigré artists living in Prague establish the Oskar Kokoschka Association. Its members include Theo Balden and John Heartfield, and the group's objective is to 'preserve' a 'genuinely humanistic and progressive German art'. OK himself does not join.

The sufferings of the Spanish people in the Civil War prompt him to produce the coloured lithograph 'Help the Basque Children', which is placarded in Prague and several other Bohemian cities.

Works on the picture he began in Dresden and continued in Paris, 'The Fountain'. The female figure is now given the features of Olda Palkovská.

Autumn: September: Begins 'Portrait of a "Degenerate Artist"' in the house of Olda Palkovská's grandparents at Ostravice. Finishes it at Wittkowitz, Moravian Ostrava, in the house of Professor Emil Korner, the brother of a childhood friend from Vienna. Kidney trouble forces him to spend a few days in the surgical ward of the industrial infirmary at Wittkowitz.

In *A World History of Art* Sheldon Warren Cheney points out OK's importance.

Poster 'Help the Basque Children!' 1937

POMOZTE BASKICKÝM DĚTEM!

1938

1938

12 February: Hitler receives the Austrian Chancellor Schuschnigg at Berchtesgaden and threatens a military invasion of Czechoslovakia. OK drafts a spontaneous 'Request to the Court of Arbitration in The Hague, for an assessment of the unconstitutional state of affairs in Austria under the regime of Herr von Schuschnigg.'

12 March: invasion of Austria by German troops. 13 March: Austria's *Anschluss* to Germany. OK writes to Ehrenstein: 'As far as I'm concerned, I shan't leave Prague as long as there is an immediate threat of war. Firstly, because of my sister, who is not well, but also because I don't feel like it . . . Unfortunately I've exhausted my supply of Maecenases . . .' (Spring). Financial problems.

Spring: The German Reich Propaganda Ministry offers art dealers both inside Germany and abroad twenty-four of OK's oil paintings to sell. Among them are 'Les Dents du Midi', 'The Trance Player', 'Woman in Blue' and 'London, Tower Bridge'.

Summer: 1 July: Dismissed from the Prussian Academy of Arts. 7 July: in London the first substantial exhibition of *20th Century German Art* opens (New Burlington Galleries, 7–31 July). OK represented by nineteen works, including the 'Portrait of a "Degenerate Artist"'. The first book on modern German art to be published in England appears (Oto Bihalji-Merin, alias Peter Thoene, *Modern German Art*), in which OK is presented as a major figure. In Prague starts work on the picture 'Summer II (Zrání)'.

September: First one-man show in U.S.A., at the Buchholz Gallery, New York. 29 September: the Munich Accord, whereby Hitler, Mussolini, Chamberlain and Daladier sign a document which obliges the government in Prague to cede the Sudetenland to the German Reich by 10 October. OK comments to Ehrenstein: 'for this Gestapo gang will still be with us when the whole of Europe has willingly handed itself over to Moscow. And that will be the end of European wisdom and intelligence – these governments today are more stupid than any that has ever existed in past generations.'

October: Olda Palkovská urges OK to leave Prague, and attempts to get aeroplane tickets. Establishes friendly links with the married couple Ruth and Adolf Arndt in Switzerland; they become his most reliable connection with the continent in the following difficult years. OK to Arndt: 'I want to get away from here at once, because I can't work here any more. I've had my cases packed for a couple of weeks now. The only problem is transport – by air, needless to say. Because

of a moratorium on 'plane tickets they're not on sale for the time being' (5 October).

18 October: leaves Prague with Olda Palkovská; flies via Rotterdam to London, taking the unfinished picture 'Zrání' in his luggage. At first they stay in a boarding-house at 11a Belsize Avenue, then from 31 October at 45a King Henry's Road, NW3. Emil Korner gives them £100. OK writes to Arndt: '. . . after my initial panic I've now had my eyes opened to the beauty of the world. I'll have to scrape a living for a while, but then things will be all right . . . yesterday Sir Kenneth Clark, Director of the National Gallery, urged me to stay here no matter what, and he'll make all the arrangements for me. Today I've been invited to tea with the Director of the Tate Gallery, Rothenstein, who is also championing my work, and tomorrow I go to the Courtauld Institute' (20 October). For the time being, however, the recognition he hopes to get from the British public eludes him.

From memory paints a last view of Prague, ('Prague, Nostalgia'). Makes contact with the Artists' Refugee Committee in Hampstead (47, Downshire Hill).

December: takes part in the initially unofficial foundation of the Free German League of Culture at the house of the emigré German lawyer, Fred Uhlman. Thanks to Uhlman obtains his first commission to paint the portrait of Michael Croft (Uhlman's brother-in-law).

1939

January: 'Zrání' included in the exhibition *Living Art in England*, at the London Gallery.

9 February: gives a television interview at Broadcasting House, Alexandra Palace.

1 March: official foundation of the Free German League of Culture (F.D.K.B.), soon to become the most active organization of the German-speaking emigrant community in Britain. Members include John Heartfield, the critic Alfred Kerr, the writer Stefan Zweig, and OK. The Church of England makes a meeting house at 36a Upper Park Road available to the group.

13 March: foundation of the Austrian Centre-Association of Austrians, with a club-house in Paddington, at 126, Westbourne Terrace, W2; honorary president Sigmund Freud. OK occasionally attends performances at the 'Laterndl', the club theatre of the Austrian Centre.

April: the St. Etienne Gallery in Paris exhibits several portraits and one critic describes OK as 'a visionary from the family of Grünewald' (*Beaux Arts*).

12 May: at the F.D.K.B. event 'Creative Exiles' reads from his own works.

Spring/early summer: paints the portrait of 'Posy Croft', Michael Croft's sister.

20 June: opening of the first *F.D.K.B. Exhibition* at the Wertheim Gallery. OK represented by the portrait of Michael Croft, 'Zrání', 'Prague, Nostalgia' and the 'Portrait of a "Degenerate Artist"'.

30 June: at the Fischer Galleries in Lucerne pictures confiscated from German museums are sold by auction. Nine oils by OK sold abroad, including 'The Trance Player' (2,100 Fr.), 'Duchess of Montesquiou' (3,000 Fr.). The Kunstmuseum Basle acquires 'The Tempest' from the picture-depot of the Ministry of Propaganda in Berlin for 4,000 Fr.

July: contributes to the *Exhibition of the Austrian Centre-Association of Austrians* at 126 Westbourne Terrace W2.

9 August: with Olda moves to Polperro in Cornwall, where the sculptor Uli Nimptsch is living. From 28 August lives at Cliff End Cottage. Paints the landscapes 'Polperro I' and 'II' from the terrace of the house, and a series of watercolours.

3 September: England declares war on Germany. Starts work on the two allegories 'The Crab' and 'Private Property', which represent his first comments on the current political situation. More work on the play *Comenius*.

1940

January: an increasingly positive response in America, with an exhibition at the St. Etienne Gallery, New York (9 January–2 February).

Summer: in June the South Coast of England is declared a prohibited area for foreigners. Nimptsch is interned. July: OK and Olda return to London. They stay initially at the Strand Palace Hotel; with the help of Kathleen, Countess of Drogheda, from 18 July they rent a furnished house in Boundary Road. OK paints a large number of flower pieces in watercolour. Supports the F.D.K.B. and the Austrian Centre in their attempts to revoke Parliament's legislation dividing refugees into 'enemy or friendly aliens', which results in many of the former being interned. As Czech citizens, he and Olda are classified among the latter.

September: from 6 September onwards regular German air-raids until April 1941.

Autumn: Edith Hoffmann has her first conversations with OK in preparation for her biography. Finishes 'Private Property', in which he interprets capitalist greed as one of the causes of impending disaster.

Winter: starts work on his third political oil 'The Red Egg', in which he depicts the Munich Accord 'as a bacchanalian orgy . . . to satisfy the Imperialists' hunger for power' (D. Schmidt). At a Christmas recitation of the F.D.K.B. reads his short story 'About the Girl Libussa'.

1941

January: exhibition at the Arts Club, Chicago (twenty-three pictures and graphic works).

29 January: moves to 11, Mandeville Court, Finchley Road. Finishes 'The Red Egg'.

February: Edvard Beneš, former President of the Czechoslovak Republic and head of the Government in Exile, donates the painting 'Polperro II' to the Tate Gallery.

15 May: marries Olda Palkovská in an air-raid shelter, the temporary Hampstead registry office. Nimptsch and his wife are witnesses.

Starts work on his fourth political picture 'Loreley', which depicts the atrocities of naval warfare. Paints several watercolours, including a portrait of the artist Marie-Louise von Motesiczky.

Summer: becomes President of the F.D.K.B., and retains this post until 1946. On his initiative the F.D.K.B. shows an international exhibition of children's art in August. 16 August: makes the opening address at the *Children's Art Exhibition*.

Autumn: 4 September–30 October: in S.W. Scotland with Olda, stays at the House of Elrig, near Port William, Wigtownshire as guest of the Korner family. Paints the landscape 'Scottish Coast' and produces watercolours and his first coloured pencil drawings. According to Olda's memoirs: 'We often used to go for long walks, he always. taking a drawing-block and a packet of pencils in his pocket. In the gentle, hilly landscape

Polperro: Cliff End Cottage is the second house from the top

Olda Palkovská, Polperro, 1939 or 1940

The House of Elrig: Kokoschka's rooms on the first floor

near the south-western coast of Scotland he used to draw cows and sheep, and the broad vistas across the land and sea.'

27 October–15 November: the Buchholz Gallery, New York exhibits twenty-five oils.

13 December: foundation of the Free Austrian Movement which advocates the restoration of a free and independent Austria. OK joins and gives special support to Young Austria, its youth section. Promises to make this section an annual donation from the proceeds of picture sales.

22 December: in the periodical *Zeitspiegel – Anti-Nazi Weekly* demands the release of Austrians interned in English camps.

1942
January: writes the essay 'Die Wahrheit ist unteilbar' (The Truth is Indivisible); published in February in the periodical of the F.D.K.B. (*Freie Deutsche Kultur – German Anti-Nazi Monthly*). It is an appeal to German emigrants to participate in the creation of a new democracy: 'The earth will be cleansed of the crimes, cleansed of the curse which has been visited on mankind – this is what democracy demands. Like liberty, the truth is indivisible.'

February: in an open letter to *Zeitspiegel* in London, expresses his views on the educative role of theatre, which should not merely entertain but show the spectator 'how to become human'.

March: represented at the exhibition *Czecho-Slovak Contemporary Art* at the Demotte Gallery, New York. Invited to paint the portrait of the Soviet Ambassador to London, Ivan Maisky. First sitting on 19 March. Donates the fee (to the value of £1,000) for this commission, completed in 1943, to the Stalingrad Hospital Fund. Works on the oil 'Marianne-Maquis', which attacks the Allies' tardiness in opening up a Second Front. At the same time paints 'Anschluss – Alice in Wonderland'.

Summer: gives several lectures, including one on 11 June to open the *Anti-Nazi Committee Exhibition*, a speech for the 'Opening of the Institute for Science and Learning of the Free German League of Culture' (June/July), as well as an address given during the Soviet-Austrian friendship week (20/21 June). Regarding the latter he notes: 'Result of the Collection: £3,600 for X-ray unit sent to the Russian Army'.

6 August–2 October: second stay at Elrig. Paints watercolours of duck, pheasant, fish and mushrooms, and makes coloured pencil drawings.

October: given permission through Sir Kenneth Clark to paint from the roof of Unilever House, London; begins a view of St. Paul's though the picture remains unfinished, since the constant supervision disturbs his concentration.

One-man show at the City Art Museum, St. Louis, with thirty-eight works.

25 October: as President of the F.D.K.B. gives an address in the Conway Hall to mark the 25th anniversary of the Soviet Union, and in it praises the new social system in Russia. This speech causes some ill-feeling amongst the membership of the F.D.K.B., but OK defends himself against the charge of his 'excessively left-wing political outlook' as follows: 'I have never had party-political views... But I do feel duty-bound to speak my mind whenever my reason and conscience prompt me to do my utmost for a good cause. This is a case in point, for we are promoting or defending German culture' (9 November).

Member of the German Refugees Committee.

November: the *Burlington Magazine* publishes his article 'An Approach to the Baroque Art of Czechoslovakia' (written in 1938). In its anthology *Teacher of Nations – Addresses and Essays* the Cambridge University Press publishes his article 'Comenius, The English Revolution and our Present Plight'.

The Government of Czechoslovakia in Exile (Beneš) donates the painting 'Zrání' to the National Gallery of Scotland.

1943
5 January: gives an address to open the exhibition *The War as Seen by Children* at the Cooling Galleries, London (text published in the exhibition catalogue).

18 February: under the title 'Und sie bewegt sich doch' writes the foreword to the volume *Free German*

Port William, Wigtownshire

Elrig, late summer 1942

Writing, published in London by the Free German Youth Press. Paints 'What we are fighting for' as his contribution to the exhibition *For Liberty* organized by the A.I.A. (Artists' International Association).

13 March–11 April: *For Liberty* held in the new basement canteen near the bombed-out portion of John Lewis, behind Oxford Street.

31 March–24 April: the St. Etienne Gallery in New York exhibits *Oskar Kokoschka: Aspects of his Art*.

In letters to Arndt which often betray desperation, OK anxiously tries to find out what has become of his brother in Vienna.

2–29 April: stays at Nevin (Nanhoron Arms Hotel) on the west coast of Caernarvonshire, N. Wales, with the painter, later photographer, Edwin Smith. Produces several sketches in coloured pencil.

Summer: 10 July at the opening of the F.D.K.B. theatre in Hampstead makes a speech ('A Great Task'), on the question of the re-education of Nazi youth in Germany after the war.

2–30 September: second visit to Nevin. Henry Dreyfus is persuaded by Edward Beddington-Behrens to buy and present the portrait of Maisky to the Tate Gallery.

6 December: moves to Flat 168, 55 Park Lane. Able to use as a studio an attic room in the house at 99, Park Lane, which Beddington-Behrens makes available to him. Several visits to Music Hall (The Old Bedford) with Edwin Smith.

19 December: makes a speech to mark the fifth anniversary of the F.D.K.B. Paints 'Capriccio' and 'Duck Shooting'. Starts work on the portrait 'Evelyn [Threnody]'.

1944

15–16 January: takes part in the Free German Cultural Convention at Caxton Hall, London.

Spring: 4 April–15 May: third visit to Elrig, where he produces more drawings in coloured pencil and starts work on the oil 'Scottish Landscape with Sheep' (completed in London in 1945).

20 April: from Scotland telegraphs the Czech Embassy in London, where a conference of foreign artists is discussing artists' political tasks in post-war Europe: 'The urgent task of the artists at present is to make society conscious of the fact that culture affects the life, freedom and happiness of every individual . . . We artists have a responsibility towards the young generation of Europe, which has all reasons to doubt justice and to believe that Power Politics and ruthless force will be the bitter truth again hidden behind all the nice talks . . . we artists must by no means dare to be indulgent. Our duty is to be honestly critical of everybody and everything at present.'

27 May: Impressed by a production of Kleist's *Amphitryon* at the F.D.K.B. theatre in Hampstead, writes to the organizers: '. . . a mission to spread the idea of genuine liberty, which gives the human ego a breath of the divine . . . Beyond the massed battles which are now being fought, more penetrating than their deafening noise, and quite different in kind from the corruption and the ghastly stench of blood which hangs over our age, was the enchanting appeal of liberty that I heard spoken yesterday evening from the stage of the Free German Cultural Association' (28 May).

Masaryk portrait sold in New York. Out of the proceeds OK donates 4,000 dollars to the newly established Oskar Kokoschka Fund for War Orphans of all Nations United in Liberated Czechoslovakia.

In the F.D.K.B. periodical writes 'On Expressionism' on the occasion of an exhibition of modern Continental art at the Leicester Galleries.

Summer: contributes 'What we are fighting for' to an A.I.A. exhibition of German art at the Charlotte Street Centre, London (8–28 June). Writes the foreword to the catalogue of *Free German Artists*; also the preface to the catalogue of an exhibition of works by Edwin Smith at the Berkeley Galleries.

From June onwards concerted air-raids by flying-bombs (V1s and later V2s) on London. The Kokoschkas have a narrow escape.

6 July–9 August: Travels to N.W. Scotland and stays at Ullapool, Ross-shire (Royal Hotel). Friendship with Constance Mitford. Hot weather. Numerous coloured pencil drawings of the landscape, animals, fish, fruit, flowers etc.

10 August–26 September: fourth visit to Elrig. Continuing fine weather. Paints 'The Hunters' – 'some queer neighbours here, hunting and shooting people in eerie overgrown houses without anybody to look after them . . . I do not see how they all do not die in winter of rheumatism and lumbago' (Olda to Constance Mitford, 20 September); as well as the portrait of a 15-year-old Scottish girl, 'Minona'.

Autumn: in London, starts work on the portrait 'Kathleen, Countess of Drogheda'. *Der Sturm* exhibition at the Kunstmuseum, Berne (October 1944–March 1945): OK represented by twenty-two works.

Winter: frequent visits to the Old Vic to see performances of Ibsen, Chekhov, Shakespeare and Shaw: 'the best theatre . . . ever' (Olda to Constance Mitford, 31 December).

1945

Spring: *Apropos* no. 3 publishes his article 'The Portrait in the Past and Present'.

5–20 April: stays at Dartington Hall, near Totnes, Devon. Visits Colonel Norman Colville, near Launceston, Cornwall.

7 May: Germany's unconditional surrender. Writes article 'The Essence of Austrian Culture' in response to the devastation the War has caused in Europe.

June: writes the foreword to Hans Tietze's *Outline of a History of Austrian Art* (Junges Österreich-Jugend Voran Press) as an appeal to the victorious Powers to maintain cultural traditions in Austria.

Autumn: 14 August–10 September: fifth visit to Elrig. Watercolours and drawings. 10 September: travels on to Ullapool (The Old Manse, then Royal Hotel). Begins the oil 'Ullapool' (completed later in London owing to bad weather). The Kokoschkas return by train via Insch, Aberdeen and Edinburgh, where they spend two days, mostly in the National Gallery with its director Stanley Cursiter. '. . . they have some wonderful things there. Altogether we liked the town very much, the stone-built houses and squares, and the lovely high rooms, it was a pity we

Poster, 1945

236

were so unlucky with the weather' (Olda to Constance Mitford).

15 September–1 November: the Neue Galerie in Vienna shows twenty-three drawings and prints in its exhibition *Klimt, Schiele, Kokoschka*. J.P. Hodin publishes an article on OK in *New Writing and Daylight* (September).

Winter: a month before Christmas has 5,000 posters put up in London Underground stations with the caption 'In Memory of the Children of Europe who have to die of cold and hunger this Christmas'. Donates £1,000 to a fund for Viennese children.

Writes the foreword, 'German Artists in England' to a series of reproductions of works by F.D.K.B. artists.

December: writes the 'Petition from a Foreign Artist to the Righteous People of Britain for a Secure and Present Peace', his last political statement of the war years for Edith Hoffmann's biography, as a warning against the loss of spiritual and moral values in a world dominated by technological progress and the dangers of the atom bomb.

In the *Magazine of Arts*, New York, Alfred Neumeyer writes a long article about OK.

Study for Christmas Card, 1945

1946

Works on 'Kathleen, Countess of Drogheda', 'Acrobat's Family', 'The Unleashing of Atomic Energy' and 'Goddess Flying'.

1 March: to mark his sixtieth birthday, is honoured by Vienna in a number of ways; the Mayor, Theodor Körner, sends him a long telegram exhorting him to come 'home' and take part in the re-organization of the School of Applied Arts.

May: writes the essay 'Of Seeing and Hearing'.

Summer: June: moves to 120 Eyre Court, Finchley Road, into a flat which from September 1940 onwards had been occupied by Olda's parents.

July: 22 July–10 September: last visit to Elrig, where he produces the series of 'Constance' drawings.

22 October: flies to Prague for the funeral of his brother-in-law, Emil Patocká.

November: 18 November–28 December: *Exposition International d'Art Moderne*, organized by Unesco at the Museum of Modern Art, in Paris. Represented by four pictures from Edward Beddington-Behrens's collection ('Evelyn', 'The Crab', 'Capriccio', 'What we are fighting for').

In Buenos Aires Hans Platschek's monograph *Oskar Kokoschka* appears.

1947

February: takes British citizenship. Preparations for a retrospective at the Kunstmuseum Basle.

March: travels to Basle, for the exhibition which opens on 22 March containing sixty-five paintings, 153 watercolours and drawings, and forty-two lithographs. Gives a lecture, to open the exhibition, on 'Bild, Sprache und Schrift' (Image, Language and Script). The exhibition is widely appreciated; *Die Zeit* publishes a long article called 'The Painter with the X-Ray Eyes'. Signs several contracts for publications of his works in books, portfolios and periodicals.

April: visits Tessin, Astano and Gandria.

Summer: from 1 May onwards in Sierre (Hôtel du Chateau). With some interruptions remains here until October. Paints the landscapes 'Vineyards near Sion' and 'Tourbillon de Sion'. In the grounds of the castle of Muzot, begins the portrait of the industrialist Werner Reinhart, brother of the Swiss art collector, Oskar Reinhart. Edith Hoffmann's *Oskar Kokoschka – Life and Work* published by Faber and Faber. In *The Spectator* (20 June) Lawrence Gowing praises it as 'the best study of a living painter that has appeared for many years'.

July: in *Il Mondo Europeo* Michelangelo Masciotta writes about 'Le Ultime Pitture di Oskar Kokoschka' (1 July). 2 July: the *Neue Zürcher*

Zeitung prints Kokoschka's short story 'The Story of our Daughter Virginia'; and on the 8th, 9th, 10th, and 13th of the month the same newspaper publishes his short story 'Kinderkrankheit' (Children's Illness). 4 July: in Zurich, for the opening of his exhibition at the Kunsthaus (sixty-nine paintings, 109 watercolours and drawings; 4 July–31 August). On 30 August the future President of West Germany, Theodor Heuss, writes in the *Rhein-Neckar-Zeitung* on 'Developments and Changes in Oskar Kokoschka's Oeuvre'.

Attends an exhibition of late Gothic panel paintings at the Museum in Schaffhausen; subsequently writes the essay 'Old German Painting' (published 1948 in the December issue of *Atlantis*).

September: spends three weeks on the Riffel Alp near Zermatt, where he paints the landscapes 'Montana' and 'Matterhorn'. On an excursion to Leuk paints 'Landscape of Leuk and the Rhône Valley'.

October: visits his brother Bohuslav in Vienna, where, with Viktor Matejka's help, he sets about convincing Mayor Körner that the expropriated house in the Liebhartstal should be restored to the family.

Returns to London, presumably at the end of the month, and tries to obtain artificial limbs from America for young Austrians crippled in the War.

November/December: an interview with OK called 'The Father of Modern Art?' published in several newspapers (including *Der Sonntag*, 23 November). On 28 November the *Österreichisches Tagebuch* publishes his essay 'Ich bin ein Seher' (I am a Visionary).

Exhibition at the Stedelijk Museum, Amsterdam.

1948

January: tries to arrange to paint Mahatma Gandhi and after his murder on 30 January writes '. . . I was due to paint the greatest, most unassuming human being since Christ – Gandhi. I had always venerated him as the most outstanding example of humanism, and a little while ago his invitation reached me. Yet this dignified old man, who alone preached love as the antidote to universal hatred, was struck down by a bullet manufactured by that brutish process of mechanization in which our technological civilization parodies itself so grotesquely. I wept the whole day, and more or less lost the heart to raise my feeble voice any longer against this shameless age' (to E. Pisk, 13 March).

May: exhibition of work by his pupil, Ishbel McWhirter at the Starling Gallery, London; OK writes the preface to the catalogue.

Summer: 6 June travels with Olda to the

Biennale in Venice. In a special exhibition at the Biennale represented by sixteen paintings. His first major success in Italy; more than twenty-two periodicals, including *Il Tempo*, *L'Unitá*, and *Il Giornale della Sera* print critiques of his works. Once again paints the view from a window of the Europa Britannia Hotel towards Santa Maria della Salute and also paints the picture 'Venice, Bacino di San Marco'. Very impressed by Titian's late work 'Ecce Homo' in the Accademia, and in it sees a 'melancholy expression of the decay in human spirituality, which has dogged mankind since ancient times'.

25 July–22 August: stays at Sirmione on Lake Garda.

Autumn: 22–27 August: stays at Cles/Tyrol. 27 August–1 September: travels via Ravenna, Bologna and Ferrara to Florence. Stays in Florence till December (1 September–17 December). Lives first at Fiesole, where he paints the 'Self-portrait'. Subsequently at the Berdinelli Hotel by the Arno in Florence. In September paints the picture 'Florence Cathedral' and a little later 'Florence, View from the Antinori Tower'. Numerous sketches in and near Florence, including one of the bronze figures of the Neptune Fountain in front of the Palazzo Vecchio.

October: James S. Plaut from the Institute of Contemporary Art in Boston organizes a major exhibition, shown first at Boston (16 October–14

Venice, summer 1948

November) and also in Washington (5 December–17 January), St. Louis (21 February–21 March), San Francisco (10 April–15 May), Wilmington (6 June–3 July) and New York (19 July–4 October) – OK's first major exhibition outside Europe.

December: in Florence greatly admires Michelangelo's works, and writes to Marcel Ray: 'Yesterday tears came to my eyes, as I unexpectedly found myself standing before Michelangelo's sarcophagus in the Church of San Lorenzo. I realized for the first time that this God among artists is dead' (5 December). Paints the portrait of the Archbishop of Florence, 'Cardinal dalla Costa'. 18 December: returns via Vienna to London. Subsequently writes the essay 'Visit to Post-War Italy'.

An expanded version of the exhibition catalogue *Oskar Kokoschka* by James S. Plaut published in England and America.

1949
January: in *Horizon*, J.P. Hodin publishes an article on 'Expressionism' with illustrations of OK's work.

Spring: February/March: in New York, Hugo Feigl exhibits watercolours. Seven pictures are shown at the St. Etienne Gallery (March–April).

April: OK travels to Zurich (12 April) and Vienna. Paints the portrait of the Mayor of Vienna, Theodor Körner.

5 May: to Rome with Olda. From the Palatine Hill paints the view towards the 'Forum Romanum' and in June the 'Colosseum'. Sketches numerous works of art, including the statue of Marcus Aurelius on the Capitol, and Bernini's sculptures. At the archaeologist Ludwig Curtius's house introduced to the conductor Wilhelm Furtwängler, who from 1953 onwards becomes his neighbour and friend.

Summer: 17 July: flies back to London. From 24 July in Boston, where he runs a summer course at the Tanglewood Summer School.

Autumn: from 13 September in Minneapolis, where he paints the couple John and Bettie Cowles. Subsequently in New York, where at the Museum of Modern Art he goes to see his touring exhibition. Returns to London on 19 November. First consultations with Count Antoine Seilern about a ceiling painting for his private residence, 56 Princes Gate, London SW7. Also makes a preliminary drawing for 'Apocalypse'.

Exhibition at the I.C.A. in London *Modern German Prints and Drawings* includes works by OK.

In Florence Masciotta's monograph *Oskar Kokoschka* appears.

1950
Spring: in London from early January to late July works on the ceiling triptych 'The Prometheus Saga' for Count Seilern. The contract for the central picture 'Apocalypse' is signed on 14 January. On 9 March agreement is reached about adding two more paintings: 'Prometheus' (right) and 'Hades and Persephone' (left-hand side). According to Kokoschka 'the picture represents the tragedy of man, who is in danger of overstepping the law laid upon him by his own nature'. At over 8 metres long, this triptych is his largest pictorial work to date.

Summer: June: Stays in Dublin. July: travels with Olda via Amsterdam and Zurich to Salzburg, where, with some interruptions, he remains until October. Paints the view over the Old City from the Capuchin Mountain ('Salzburg'). Considers settling permanently in Salzburg; with Friedrich Welz forges plans to establish an International Summer School of Art.

8 August: in Salzburg gives the lecture 'Thirteen Years after the Exhibition: *Degenerate "Art"*'.

3 September: in Munich for the opening of his retrospective at the Haus der Kunst (September/October), the first exhibition of his work in Germany since the War (shown at Hamburg November/December). For the catalogue, Wilhelm F. Arntz compiles the first list of the artist's graphics.

Autumn: October: travels via Cles/Tyrol to Florence, and makes drawings of Ammanati's figures of the Neptune Fountain. From 23 October in Rome, on 26 October travels to Naples, Pompeii (29 October) and Amalfi (1 November). Arising out of this visit, writes the essay 'The Cross in Pompeii', reflections on ancient Greek painting. Late November, back in Zurich.

1 December: in Frankfurt for the production of his drama *Orpheus and Eurydice*. Subsequently on the Victorshöhe near Bonn paints the portrait of the President of the Federal Republic, Theodor Heuss (5–16 December). Returns to London 19 December.

1951
Spring: 10–28 January: the Kunsthalle Mannheim shows the touring exhibition from Munich and Hamburg. In London OK paints the portrait of his friend Sebastian Isepp (January/February). To celebrate his 65th birthday, additional exhibitions at Schloss Charlottenburg, Berlin, with forty-three pictures (February/March), and the Wallraf-Richartz-Museum, Cologne, with thirty pictures (March/April).

April: the City of Cologne awards him the Stefan-Lochner-Medal. 25 April: short stay in

Amsterdam. From 27 April onwards, stays in Hamburg, where he paints the portrait of the Mayor, Max Brauer, and subsequently the view across the harbour as seen from the tower of the Bernhard-Nocht-Institute ('View of Hamburg Harbour I'). With Bruno Snell, Rector of Hamburg University, makes preliminary plans for a mural within the university complex.

Summer/Autumn: exhibition at the Neue Galerie in Linz (June/August). July: stays in Amsterdam, then returns to London. On 21 August back in Amsterdam, whence he drives with Olda, in a borrowed Volkswagen, via Cologne, Mannheim, Karlsruhe and Augsburg to Salzburg. On 3 September travels from Salzburg to Zurich and thence into the Engadine (from 9 September onwards). Here paints the landscape 'Maloja'. Subsequently goes on via Verona to Venice, where for the fourth time paints the church of 'Santa Maria della Salute' from his viewpoint in the Europa Britannia Hotel.

Winter: 4 November: Olda and Oskar buy a plot of land at Villeneuve, on the eastern shore of the Lake of Geneva. In Zurich begins the portrait of the industrialist and art collector Emil Bührle. Made a Freeman of his home town of Pöchlarn. 26 December: back in London. Writes the epilogue to Benno Geiger's monograph on Giuseppe Arcimboldi.

The Galerie Welz in Salzburg publishes two of the artist's *Orbis Pictus* portfolios.

1952

25 January–1 February: in Hamburg, to receive the I. Lichtwark-Prize of the Free Hanseatic City of Hamburg (26 January) to the value of 15,000 DM. Subsequently in London, where he writes the essay 'The Prometheus Saga' (later published in several periodicals, including *Das Werk*). From 20 April in Zurich, where he finishes the portrait 'Emil Bührle' and also paints those of the art dealer Walter Feilchenfeldt's two sons, and of 'Bettina Angehrn'.

Summer: returns to London, on 9 June, where he completes the drawings for *Ann Eliza Reed*. On 7 July back in Zurich; attends the major Edvard Munch exhibition at the Kunsthaus. Writes an article about it in the *Neue Zürcher Zeitung*, called 'The Expressionism of Edvard Munch' (18–20 July).

At the 26th Biennale in Venice, represented by a number of new pictures, including 'The Prometheus Saga'.

From 20 July in Salzburg, where rooms for his summer school are provisionally set aside on the Feste Hohensalzburg. Travels on to Cles (3 August) and Pontresina (until 2 September). Paints the landscape 'Pontresina'. Spends September in Zurich, then returns to London. The I.C.A. shows a number of his graphic works (10 September–10 October). Favourable review by M.H. Middleton in *The Spectator* (19 September), who demands 'a full exhibition of his [OK's] painting'.

Winter: 1 November: travels to the USA; visiting lecturer at the Minneapolis School of Art. Paints the portrait 'Pete Gale'. On 28 December returns to London. His article 'I have Deliberately Broken all Taboos' appears on 27 and 28 December in *Die Neue Zeitung*, Frankfurt. The story *Ann Eliza Reed*, together with eleven lithographs, is published by the Maximillian Press, Hamburg. Paul Westheim publishes *Oskar Kokoschka – Figures and Landscapes*.

1953

Spring: in London. Produces the first eight pen and coloured ink drawings for the 'Thermopylae' triptych. Exhibitions at the Künstlerhaus, Oslo (14 February–18 March) and in the Frankfurt Kunstkabinett (21 March–mid April).

March: to mark the centenary of Van Gogh's birth, writes the essay 'Van Gogh's Influence on Modern Painting' (published in *Mededelingen van de Dienst voor Schöne Kunst der Gemeente's Gravenhage* 1953).

28 May: at King's College, Cambridge gives a lecture 'On The Opening of the International Summer School in Salzburg'. A German version appears on 8 August as an article in the *Neue Zürcher Zeitung* entitled 'Observations about Teaching Art'.

Summer: represented in the exhibition *Masterpieces of German Art in the 20th Century* at the Museum of Art, Lucerne by eleven paintings, as well as watercolours and drawings.

10 July: travels via Zurich and Munich to Salzburg. Foundation of the International Summer School for the Visual Arts. In August gives the first class in his course The School of Seeing (Painting) on the Feste Hohensalzburg (duration of course: five weeks). Uli Nimptsch from London takes the course on sculpture, the Zurich architect Hofmann, that on architecture. Of the forty-four students enrolled, twenty-seven attend Kokoschka's course. The artist explains his aims thus: 'I am establishing this International Academy in Salzburg in order to embody the European conception of a world which surrounds all our lives as the living heritage of the past, and which at the same time confronts us all afresh in the creative activity of every talented individual . . . My school does not strive towards technical skill, nor towards photographic imitations of nature, and not at all towards abstract art. I want to teach my students the art of visions, an ability greatly lost in modern society'.

Preliminary plans with Head of Design Gustav Vargo and with Wilhelm Furtwängler for set designs for a production of Mozart's *The Magic Flute* at the Salzburg Festival.

9 September: moves into the house which they have had built at Villeneuve, directly above Lake Geneva.

1954

1 January: in Villeneuve starts work on the 'Thermopylae' triptych for Hamburg University.

Exhibitions in Santa Barbara (9 February–7 March) and San Francisco (20 March–30 April), with twenty-two paintings, and also in Rio de Janeiro (April) with eight paintings and a number of graphic works. From 2 March: back in London. Stays at the Savoy Hotel, where he paints two new Thames riverscapes: 'The New Waterloo Bridge' and 'Large Thames Landscape II'.

Summer: from 14 July in Salzburg. Takes his classes in The School of Seeing with sixty students. Giacomo Manzù (from Milan) teaches sculpture, and Clemens Holzmeister (from Vienna) architecture.

Exhibition of graphics at the Welz Gallery. Commissioned to design the set and costumes for Furtwängler's production of *The Magic Flute*.

19 August: returns to Villeneuve. Paints the cellist Pablo Casals. Completes the 'Thermopylae' triptych. A visit by the Rector of Hamburg University, Professor Kolb, the Hamburg Senator for Culture, B. Ratjen, and the former Rector, B. Snell, to view the painting.

Autumn: from 13 October in Florence. Sketches in the Bargello ('Hercules and Antaeus' by Pollaiuolo) and in the Accademia (Michelangelo's 'Slaves'). On 30 October returns to Villeneuve.

Das Werk publishes his article 'Summer School for the Fine Arts on the Hohensalzburg', and *Universitas* prints his essay 'Non-objective Art?' H.M. Wingler publishes OK's portrait drawings from the *Sturm* circle (*Artists and Poets*).

1955

Spring: works in Villeneuve on the drawings for *The Magic Flute*. Completes five lithographs for the book edition of the opera *Irish Legend* by Werner Egk.

7 April: travels via Zurich to Salzburg and Linz (Easter). From the Pfenningberg in Linz paints the view over the Danube and the city.

5 May: back in Villeneuve. Completes the picture 'Amor and Psyche' as part of the ceiling painting 'Prometheus', begun in London in 1950.

Summer: represented at the first Kassel

Documenta by a room to himself containing seven paintings including 'The Trance Player' and 'Mont Blanc'.

8 July–24 August: in Salzburg takes classes at the School of Seeing. Exhibition at the Salzburg Residenz, of his *Magic Flute* designs. Production of *The Magic Flute* in the Felsenreitschule conducted by Georg Solti. Bavarian Radio broadcasts his talk 'My Designs for *The Magic Flute*'. Welz publishes a volume containing the designs and a text by the artist, 'About the Lighting in *The Magic Flute*'.

Autumn: paints the landscape 'Villeneuve'. In September, at Sion/Wallis establishes a second School of Seeing.

Winter: 4–8 November: visits Vienna for the re-opening of the Vienna State Opera with a production of Beethoven's *Fidelio*. Sees the *Vienna Secession Exhibition*, at which he is represented by forty-eight paintings, sixty-five watercolours, and prints.

23 December: at Christmas visited by his sister Berta from Prague. Walter Kern publishes a volume about the 'Thermopylae' triptych with a text by OK.

1956
Spring: in February, from the Righi-Vaudois Hotel in Glion, paints the picture 'Glion, View of Lac Léman'. Exhibitions at the National Gallery, Prague (4–20 March), the Kunsthalle, Bremen, and the Arts Club, Chicago.

April/May: the *Schweizer Monatshefte* publishes his essay 'The Eye of Darius' about Altdorfer's 'Alexanderschlacht'. 20–25 April: travels with Olda via Venice to Athens. They hire a car and visit Corinth (1 July), Nauplia and Mycenae (2–7 July), then Delphi (7–26 July) and finally Chalkis. Between 8 July and 25 July at Delphi, from the roof of the Fine Arts Building, paints the view towards the ancient ruins ('Delphi'). Subsequently stays in Athens (27–30 July).

In the National Museum, Athens, makes numerous sketches of metopes, reliefs and vase-paintings. Later writes: 'Here I felt the same melancholy love for Greece that Goethe had for Italy.'

Summer: 2 June: returns via Venice to Vienna. Commissioned by the Ministry of Education to paint a picture of the Vienna Opera at night ('Vienna State Opera').

17–18 June: in Bonn the President of the Federal Republic presents him with the Federal Service Cross. 15 July: to celebrate Rembrandt's 350th anniversary makes a speech in the Westerkerk in Amsterdam. Then proceeds to the Summer School at Salzburg (18 July–20 August). Endows the

Oskar Kokoschka Prize, awarded annually to the student who produces the best work. 16 August: in Pöchlarn is presented with the ring of honour of the town. A celebration is held in the Carabinieri Hall at the Residenz, Salzburg for his 70th birthday. Returns to Villeneuve.

Autumn: late September, in Cologne, paints two views of the cathedral.

26 September–18 October: the School of Seeing in Sion. Produces two lithographs 'L'Enfant de Bethléhem' and 'Christ, with his Crown of Thorns' as contributions to the Fund for Hungarian Refugees.

Several publications to celebrate his 70th birthday: H.M. Wingler edits his *Writings 1907–1955*, as well as *Oskar Kokoschka – a Biographical Portrait in Contemporary Documents*; he also brings out the first catalogue raisonné of OK's paintings. Several of OK's short stories published as *Spur im Treibsand* (published in English in 1962 as *A Sea Ringed with Visions*).

1957
7–27 January: stays in Zurich and St. Moritz. The exhibition *Austrian Art* at Baden-Baden (17 January–3 February) includes twenty-three oils and lithographs.

Spring: 9 March: in the *Stuttgarter Zeitung* his article 'The Immutable Eye' published in response to a questionnaire sent out to artists and scientists on the subject of 'The Rediscovery of the Immutable'. 10 March–12 April: in London. From the balcony of Lindsey House in Cheyne Walk paints 'London, Chelsea Reach'. In the Victoria and Albert Museum makes several sketches in coloured pencils, including some of Raphael's Cartoons.

June: in Villeneuve paints 'Lake of Geneva with a Steamer'. 11 July–22 August: School of Seeing at Salzburg.

Autumn: 14–28 October: in Florence. Again makes drawings of Michelangelo's 'Slaves' in the Accademia and sketches paintings by Raphael and Rubens in the Uffizi. Returns via Bologna and Ferrara.

Winter: 20 November: travels to U.S.A., visiting New York and Minneapolis. Stays until January 1958. In Minneapolis paints portraits of 'Putnam Dana McMillan' and 'Richard P. Gale'.

1958
January: in New York paints 'The Children Richard, Margery and John Davis'. 23 January: returns to Villeneuve.

Spring: 10–16 March: in Munich attends his first major retrospective at the Haus der Kunst, with 153 paintings and 276 graphic works. In April, at

Villeneuve, paints the portrait 'Bianca Wächter'.

19 May–13 July: The Künstlerhaus in Vienna mounts the largest exhibition to date of OK's work, with a total of 682 catalogue entries.

Summer: in June, from the terrace of Furtwängler's house in Clarens, paints 'The Cedar'. 11 July–22 August: School of Seeing at Salzburg. The *Salzburger Nachrichten* prints his text 'The Conditions of Ceremonial in our Age'. Exhibition at the Gemeente Museum in The Hague (31 July–1 October).

Travels from Salzburg to Travemünde and Lübeck (28 August–12 September) where he paints 'The Jacobi Church in Lübeck'. Subsequently in Hamburg (15 September) to supervise the installation of the 'Thermopylae' triptych in the lecture hall of the Philosophical Faculty at Hamburg University. Commissioned by Axel Springer to paint the 'View from the Axel Springer House' across the city.

1959
Spring: February: in Villeneuve, paints the Albanian diplomat 'Chatin Sarachi'. In March, at Glotterbad near Freiburg, paints the Federal German Minister for Economic Affairs, Ludwig Erhard.

22 May–24 June: travels to Sicily, and stays at Positano. Exhibition at the Palazzo Barberini in Rome; awarded the Rome Prize.

Summer: Late June/early July: in Villeneuve paints 'Pamela', wife of the art historian J.P. Hodin.

13 July–14 August: to Salzburg for the School of Seeing.

Autumn: 23 September–22 November in London. In the first half of October paints the 'Large London View from Shell-Mex House' (1–13 October). Subsequently paints a portrait of the publisher Sir Stanley Unwin. Is made Commander of the British Empire.

1960
Spring: exhibition *The Late Kokoschka* at Brunswick (10 January–21 February), Bremen (28 February–10 April), Hameln (17 April–15 May), and Pforzheim (22 May–19 June). Stays in Rome from 7–13 February. From March to mid-April in Villeneuve paints the nuclear physicist Derek Jackson. From 29 April spends a week in Vienna, where he starts work on the set and costume designs for three plays by Ferdinand Raimund, performed between 1960 and 1962 at the Burgtheater, Vienna (*Moisassur's Magic Curse*, *The Captive Imagination*, and *The Ominous Crown*).

15 May–3 June: paints a view of Stuttgart.

Summer: July: in Villeneuve writes the essay

'Franz Anton Maulbertsch' as a foreword to Klara Garas's monograph. Until mid-August in Salzburg (School of Seeing). On 15–16 August attends the exhibition *Masterpieces of Greek Art* at the Kunstmuseum, Basle. Completes twelve drawings of the 'Kouros from Syracuse'. Autumn: 20 October in Copenhagen, with Chagall, awarded the International Erasmus Prize. 24 October–16 December: stays in London; paints Israel Sieff, later Lord Sieff of Brimpton. On 6 November his sister Berta dies in Prague. 8 November opening of *Kokoschka in England and Scotland* at the Marlborough Gallery, London, which is widely appreciated by the English press.

Given an honorary doctorate by Oxford University.

1961

Spring: for the *Stuttgarter Zeitung* writes the article 'I Paint Portraits because that is what I can Do' (4 February). Late February to 3 March stays in Paris. Subsequently in Vienna (13–23 March) to supervise the set and designs for the Raimund plays.

Summer: stays in Hamburg (11–21 June). Paints the view across the harbour from a crane in the Stülcken Wharf; and two views of the city ('Hamburg III' and 'Hamburg IV'), commissioned by the collectors Wilhelm Reinhold and Edgar Horstmann. From 23 June in Bremen works on the 'Market Place, Bremen'. Returns to Villeneuve (11 July). Summer School in Salzburg (20 July–12 August); awarded the ring of honour of the City of Salzburg.

Autumn: travels to Greece (1 October–13 November). From 2–8 October stays at Athens; in

the National Museum makes sketches of ancient funerary steles and sculptures, and draws the Propylaea on the Acropolis. Visits Delphi (9 October), Olympia (14 October), Sparta (17 October), Cape Sunion (21 October), and Agina (23–30 October; draws the Temple of Aphaia). Flies back to Geneva on 12 November. The drawings made in Greece serve as the originals for the lithographic portfolio *Bekenntnis zu Hellas* (Homage to Hellas).

29 December: under the heading 'Your Greatest Artistic Experience' writes an article in the *Neue Zürcher Zeitung* about his impressions of Greece.

1962

Spring: 9 February travels to Hamburg, to print the lithographs for the Greece portfolio. Shortly afterwards, the city is flooded by a storm-tide. The catastrophe makes a profound impact on OK who subsequently paints the picture 'Storm-tide in Hamburg'. Mid-March returns to Villeneuve. Early April goes back to the Burgtheater, Vienna for consultations on the set designs for Raimund's *The Captive Imagination*. Late April till 7 June in London; in May paints 'View of the Thames from the Vickers Tower'.

Summer: at Villeneuve paints the portrait 'Rudolph Palumbo' (15–30 June). To Salzburg for the 'School of Seeing' (22 July–18 August).

Autumn: in September stays in London (8–22 September) for the opening of his major retrospective at the Tate Gallery (13 September): 161 oils, 62 watercolours and drawings, and 40 graphics. The periodicals *Apollo*, *Burlington Magazine* and *Studio* all print lengthy appreciations.

1963

1 January: begins the 'Self-portrait with Olda'.

Spring: works on drawings for the portfolio *King Lear*, published in London (sixteen lithographs with the English text of Shakespeare's drama).

April: stays in Florence, where he designs costumes and sets for Verdi's *Ballo in Maschera* at the Maggio Musicale Fiorentino (première 10 May). Travels with Olda to Apulia (12 May). Visits Orvieto, Naples, Paestum, Foggia, Bari, Taranto, Gallipoli and Brindisi. Returns via Milan on 1–2 June.

For OK Apulia is 'the gateway to the ancient world, not Constantinople'. Numerous drawings. The landscape and ancient works of art inspire him to create the lithographic cycle *The Odyssey*.

Summer: in London starts work on the 'View of the Thames with Tower Bridge' (23 June–1 July). For the last time supervises his School of Seeing at Salzburg (19 July–17 August).

Autumn: from 6 October onwards, back in London, where he completes his Thames riverscape and paints the portrait of 'Countess Margerita Thurn'. In Oxford given the American Academy Award honorary doctorate.

1964

Spring: March/April: in London begins to sketch out set and costume designs for *The Magic Flute* at Covent Garden. From 21 April–8 May paints the southern German city of Freiburg. Negotiations with Covent Garden come to nothing.

December: in Villeneuve makes drawings of Ezra Pound.

Marlborough Fine Art in London bring out the large-scale lithographic cycle *Homage to Hellas*. Takes part in the Kassel *Documenta*, and at the Guggenheim Museum in New York represented in the exhibition *Van Gogh and Expressionism*. Contributes to the exhibition *L'Espressionismo-Pittura-Scultura-Architettura* at the Palazzo Strozzi in Florence.

1965

Spring: travels to Morocco (30 January–1 March). Makes drawings which serve as the originals for the later lithograph series *Marrakesh*. 28 April: in Hamburg for the opening of the exhibition of his stage designs, posters and portfolios at the Museum of Arts and Crafts. 18–22 May: stays in Florence.

Autumn: 2–4 September: attends the Lucerne Festival, where he draws the portrait of the pianist Sviatoslav Richter. Subsequently, in Villeneuve, completes the sketches begun in London for *The Magic Flute*, for a production at the Grand Théâtre in Geneva (first night: 19 October). 14–19

At his Tate Gallery exhibition, September 1962, in front of 'Mandrill'

December stays in Paris.

Marlborough Fine Art, London, publishes the lithographic portfolio *The Odyssey*: with a total of forty-four lithographs, his most comprehensive graphic cycle to date.

1966
Spring: 1 January starts work on the painting 'Saul and David'. 13 February–20 March: travels to Puerto d'Andraix, Majorca. Awarded a number of honours to celebrate his 80th birthday. The Marlborough Gallery in London mounts the exhibition *Homage to Oskar Kokoschka*; the Staatsgalerie, Stuttgart shows *Oskar Kokoschka – Watercolours and Drawings*. In April at Cadenabbia, Italy, paints the portrait of the first Chancellor of the Federal Republic of Germany, Konrad Adenauer (1–21 April). Donates his fee to a Home for Orphaned Children in Bonn/Bad-Godesberg. At Villeneuve starts work on 'The Rejected Lover'.

Summer: 1 June: in Zurich, for the opening of his major retrospective at the Kunsthaus (*Oskar Kokoschka*, 221 works). Travels to The Hague and Amsterdam to see a Vermeer Exhibition (26 June–1 July). 12 August: in Berlin commissioned by Axel Springer five years after the erection of the Wall, to paint the view across the still largely devastated heart of Berlin. Exhibition at the Kunstverein Karlsruhe: *Oskar Kokoschka – The Portrait* (21 August–20 November).

Autumn: from Berlin to Rotterdam, and from there by ship to New York (September–11 November). Paints 'New York, Manhattan with the Empire State Building'. Exhibition at the Marlborough-Gerson Gallery (October/November). After his return to Villeneuve begins

the lithographic cycle *Saul and David*.

Marlborough Fine Art in London publishes the *Marrakesh* portfolio.

1967
Spring: travels to Libya (from 9 February onwards) and Tunisia (16 February–10 March). In April in London paints his ninth Thames riverscape, a view from the Shell Centre towards the Houses of Parliament. In a motorboat on the Thames makes several drawings of the city – the originals for the lithographic series *London from the River Thames* (published in 1967).

Autumn: stays at Gstaad, Switzerland (landscape 'Gstaad'). From October to February 1968 works at Villeneuve on the preliminary drawings for the etching cycle *The Frogs*, a title chosen to evoke the play by Aristophanes and as a reference to the establishment of a military dictatorship in Greece.

1968
Spring: in March, travels to Turkey, visiting Istanbul (15 March), Antalya (24 March) and Izmir. Travels on by Volkswagen to Bergama, Ephesus, Miletus and Didyma. Returns to Istanbul, where at the flat occupied by the Director of the German Archaeological Institute, Professor Rudolf Naumann, paints the view over the Bosphorus, 'Istanbul II' (4–20 April).

Summer: at Villeneuve completes the painting 'The Frogs' begun in February, and writes on the back: 'Europa's-Sunset 1968 – Prague 23.8.68', a reference to the invasion of Prague by Russian tanks.

November: stays in Madrid, to visit the Prado (11–17 November).

1969
Spring: 28 April–17 May: in London, where he paints the portrait of Agatha Christie. The Marlborough Gallery shows the new graphic series *Saul and David*, *Le Bal Masqué* and *The Frogs*. In early summer works at Villeneuve on the etchings for Heinrich von Kleist's tragedy *Penthesilea*.

Summer: near Edinburgh paints the double-portrait 'The Duke and Duchess of Hamilton' (7–30 July).

Autumn: travels to Greece and Cyprus, visiting Athens (14 October), Nicosia and Famegusta (20 October–13 November).

Marlborough Fine Art publishes the *Saul and David* portfolio. *The Frogs* is published by Ars Librorum, Frankfurt.

1970
At Villeneuve in February begins writing his autobiography. In June attends the opening of *Oskar Kokoschka – Drawings, Prints and Tapestries 1965–70* at the Museum of Arts and Crafts in Hamburg (25 June). Proceeds to London (27 June–22 July), where he paints the city for the last time ('London, View with St. Paul's'). Elected an honorary member of the Royal Academy.

Ars Librorum in Frankfurt bring out a boxed edition of the ten etchings for *Penthesilea* together with the text of Kleist's tragedy.

1971
Spring: in February travels to the island of Djerba, Tunisia (20 February–13 March). Subsequently in Rome (until 19 March).

To celebrate his 85th birthday, a major retrospective at the Upper Belvedere, Vienna; OK is in Vienna for the opening (27 April).

Summer: stays at Gsteig (24–28 May) and Vienna (3–10 June). The Haus der Kunst in Munich mounts the exhibition *Oskar Kokoschka – Portraits from 1907 to 1970* which OK visits in September (in Munich 12–15 September).

Winter: at Villeneuve starts work on the self-portrait 'Time, Gentlemen Please'.

1972
Spring: temporary illness. On Good Friday (31 March) completes the first cartoon for the mosaic 'Ecce Homo', for the St. Nicolai Church in Hamburg. Reads through his own writings, especially the drama *Comenius*, begun in 1935–36. In April and May travels to Greece, visiting Athens, Delphi, Olympia, Bassae and Nauplia (31 April–28 May), and makes several drawings.

Summer: works on the second mosaic cartoon 'Ecce Homines'. Stays at Gsteig (August).

With Konrad Adenauer, April 1966

Autumn/Winter: travels through Burgundy (9–17 October). At Villeneuve begins one of his last oil paintings 'Peer Gynt', after the hero of Ibsen's play. Draws 'The Women of Troy', based on the tragedy *The Trojan Women* by Euripides.

The *Florentine Sketchbook* is published.

1973

Spring: March: travels to Jerusalem (15–22 March). For the Jerusalem Foundation draws the portraits of 'Golda Meir, Prime Minister', 'Dr Shimon Agranat' (President of the Supreme Court), 'His Beatitude Benedictos I, Greek Orthodox Patriach of Jerusalem', 'Moshe Dayan, Minister of Defence', 'Sheikh Mustafa Khalil el-Ansari, Chief Warden of the Mosque of Omar', and 'Teddy Kollek, Mayor of Jerusalem'.

April/May: travels to Southern Italy (30 April–28 May) and visits Reggio, Sicily, Messina, Syracuse, Agrigento, Selinunto and Palermo.

Summer: in June preliminary discussions with Gyula Trebitsch about filming his drama *Comenius*; sketches the set designs. In Hamburg the first volume of *Oskar Kokoschka: Das schriftliche Werk* (the Literary Work), edited by Heinz Spielmann, is published, containing poems and plays. OK reads through and expands his short stories.

14 July: opening of the Oskar Kokoschka Documentary Archive, Pöchlarn, in the house where the artist was born. August: first footage for *Comenius* shot.

In London, the lithographic portfolio *The Women of Troy* published.

1974

Spring: February: travels to Madeira (8 February–7 March).

April: in Hamburg, delivers the mosaic 'Ecce Homines' to the Church of St Nicolai (8–17 April). May: an eye infection severely impairs his sight. Checks through and proof-reads his essays for publication.

Autumn: in Hamburg supervises the filming of *Comenius*.

In London the lithographic portfolio *Jerusalem Faces* appears, with the fee going to the Jerusalem Foundation. In Hamburg the second volume of his *Literary Work*, containing the short stories, is published. Publication of the English translation of his autobiography *My Life*.

1975

Spring: 28 January: cataract operation at Lausanne. Henceforth severely handicapped in his creative work. 1 March: première of the television film of *Comenius*, on ZDF, directed by Stanislav Barabas. The Austrian Chancellor Bruno Kreisky personally tries to persuade OK to reassume Austrian nationality.

July: works on the drawings for the two lithographic cycles *Comenius* and *Pan*. In Salzburg the Welz Press publishes *Oskar Kokoschka. Das druckgraphische Werk*, compiled by H.M. Wingler and Friedrich Welz, with an index of all prints completed before 1975.

1976

Spring: deeply shocked by the death of his younger brother, Bohuslav, on 12 January. March: a convalescent stay in Baden, near Zurich. Several exhibitions to celebrate his 90th birthday, including those in Salzburg (Welz), Munich (Bavarian Academy of Arts) and Athens. The Philosophical Faculty of the University of Salzburg awards him an honorary doctorate.

Summer: the Haus der Kunst in Munich exhibits the prints, *Oskar Kokoschka – Of Experience in Life* (24 July–19 September). Comprehensive retrospective at the Künstlerhaus, Bregenz (23 July–23 September).

Produces drawings for his last lithographs 'The Death of Asklepios', 'Hygieia' and 'Group (Childbed)'.

1977

Touring exhibition of the prints in Yugoslavia. With the publication of the 5th Volume, the edition of OK's drawings begun by Ernst Rathenau in 1935 is temporarily discontinued.

1978

Summer: production of Raimund's play *The Captive Imagination* presented during the Vienna Festival with set designs sketched by OK in 1960.

Major exhibition with 450 works in Japan (Kamakura, near Tokyo, and Kyoto).

Publication of his lithographs for Knut Hamsun's *Pan*. Collaborates on preparations to publish his letters.

1979

Heinz Spielmann compiles *Oskar Kokoschka. Das druckgraphische Werk II 1975–80*, as an extension to the catalogue of prints by Wingler and Welz (published in 1981).

1980

22 February: Dies in hospital at Montreux.

27 February: laid to rest in the cemetery at Clarens, near Montreux.

Villeneuve, 1973, in front of the cartoon 'Ecce Homines'

1974

Bibliography

1. Books and portfolios
   (including works illustrated by the artist).

Jagdbuch (Diarium). Vienna: Wiener Werkstätte, 1908.

Die träumenden Knaben. (The dreaming youths). Vienna: Wiener Werkstätte, 1908.

Zwanzig Zeichnungen. Berlin: Der Sturm, 1913.

Dramen und Bilder. Leipzig: Kurt Wolff, 1913. introd. by Paul Stefan. Contains the plays *Mörder Hoffnung der Frauen* (Murderer Hope of Women), *Sphinx und Strohmann* (Sphinx and Strawman) & *Schauspiel* (A play).

Mörder Hoffnung der Frauen. Berlin: Der Sturm, 1916.

Der gefesselte Kolumbus. (Columbus in chains). Berlin: Fritz Gurlitt, 1916. Portfolio of 12 lithographs illustrating Kokoschka's dramatic poem.

Menschenköpfe. (People's heads). Berlin: Der Sturm, 1916. Portfolio of 15 etchings.

O Ewigkeit – Du Donnerwort: Wörte der Kantate nach Johann Sebastian Bach. (Eternity, thou fearful word: text of Bach's Cantata). Berlin: Fritz Gurlitt, 1916 & 1917. Portfolio of 9 lithographs and poem *Zueignung* (Dedication); publ. in book-form by Fritz Gurlitt, 1918, in series 'Die Neuen Bilderbücher, l. Reihe'.

Der brennende Dornbusch; Mörder Hoffnung der Frauen. (The Burning Bush; Murderer Hope of Women). Leipzig: Kurt Wolff, 1917.

Hiob. (Job). Berlin: Paul Cassirer, 1917. Play, with 14 lithographs.

Vier Dramen. (Four plays). Berlin: Paul Cassirer, 1919. Contains the plays *Orpheus und Eurydike, Der brennende Dornbusch, Mörder Hoffnung der Frauen & Hiob*.

Der gefesselte Kolumbus. Berlin: Fritz Gurlitt (series 'Die Neuen Bilderbücher, 3. Reihe'), 1921; book edition of 1916 portfolio.

Variationen über ein Thema. Vienna: R. Lanyi; Vienna, Prague, Leipzig: Strache, 1921. introd. by Max Dvorak; ed. by Bohuslav Kokoschka. Portfolio containing 4p. text & 10 photogravure reproductions of drawings by Kokoschka.

Orpheus und Eurydice. Vienna, New York: Universal Edition, 1925. Play in 3 acts by Kokoschka, music by Ernst Křenek.

Handzeichnungen. Berlin: Rathenau, 1935. ed. by Ernest Rathenau.

Ann Eliza Reed. Hamburg: Maximilian-Presse, 1952. Story with 10 lithographs.

Schriften 1907–1955. Munich: Albert Langen-Müller, 1956. ed. by H.M. Wingler.

Thermopylae: ein Triptychon. Winterthur: BW-Presse, 1955. Text by Kokoschka & Walter Kern.

Spur in Treibsand: Geschichten. Zürich: Atlantis, 1956.

Handzeichnungen. Berlin: Rathenau, 1961. introd. by P. Westheim; ed. by Ernest Rathenau. Publ. as *Drawings*, London: Thames and Hudson, 1962.

A sea ringed with visions. London: Thames and Hudson, 1962. Stories told to Olda.

Bekenntnis zu Hellas. (Homage to Hellas). London: Marlborough Fine Art, 1964. 2 portfolios of 26 lithographs.

Apulia. London: Marlborough Fine Art, 1964. Series of 20 lithographs.

Die Odyssee. London: Ganymed Original Editions & Marlborough Fine Art, 1965. Series of 44 lithographs.

Marrakesch. London: Marlborough Fine Art, 1966. Portfolio of 18 lithographs.

Handzeichnungen/Drawings 1906–1965. New York: Ernest Rathenau, 1966; republ. Coral Gables (Fla): University of Miami Press, 1970. ed. by Ernest Rathenau; introduction by Kokoschka.

Saul und David. London: Ganymed Original Editions & Marlborough Fine Art, 1969. Series of 41 lithographs.

'Die Frösche' des Aristophanes. (Aristophanes's 'The Frogs'). Frankfurt a.M.: G. de Beauclair, 1969. Series of 12 etchings, as portfolio & in book-form.

Penthesilea. Frankfurt a.M.: G. de Beauclair, 1970. Drama by Heinrich von Kleist with 10 etchings by Kokoschka.

Saul and David. London: Thames and Hudson, 1973. Text of 2 Books of Samuel with lithographs by Kokoschka; book edition of 1969 portfolio.

Mein Leben. Munich: Bruckmann, 1971; tr. as *My Life*, London: Thames and Hudson, 1974.

Handzeichnungen 1906–1969. New York: Ernest Rathenau, 1971. introd. by Carl Georg Heise in collaboration with the artist.

The women of Troy. London: Marlborough Graphics, 1973. Series of 13 lithographs illustrating Euripides' tragedy.

Das schriftliche Werk, vols. I–IV. Hamburg: Christians, 1973–6. ed. by Hans Spielmann.

Pan. Hamburg: Hoffmann und Campe. 1978. Portfolio of 17 lithographs illustrating Knut Hamsun's novel.

Briefe I, 1905–1919. Düsseldorf: Claassen, 1984. ed. by Olda Kokoschka & Heinz Spielmann.

Briefe II, 1919–1934. Düsseldorf: Claassen, 1985. ed. by Olda Kokoschka & Heinz Spielmann.

2. Books on the artist.

Paul Westheim. *Oskar Kokoschka*. Potsdam-Berlin: Gustav Kiepenhauer, 1918.

Paul Westheim. *Oskar Kokoschka*. Berlin: Paul Cassirer, 1925.

Georg Biermann. *Oskar Kokoschka*. Leipzig, Berlin: Klinkhardt und Biermann ('Junge Kunst', Band 52), 1929.

Hans Heilmaier. *Oskar Kokoschka*. Paris: G. Grès & Cie. ('Les artistes nouveaux'), 1929.

Hans Platschek. *Oskar Kokoschka*. Buenos Aires: Poseidon ('Biblioteca Argentina de Arte'), 1946.

Edith Hoffmann. *Kokoschka : life and work*. London: Faber & Faber, 1947. incl. 2 essays by Kokoschka & a foreword by Herbert Read.

James S. Plaut. *Oskar Kokoschka*. Boston: Institute of Contemporary Art; London: Max Parrish, 1948.

Paul Westheim. *Oskar Kokoschka : Landschaften*. Zürich: Rascher, 1948.

Doris Wild. *Oskar Kokoschka : Blumenaquarelle*. Zürich: Rascher, 1948.

Michelangelo Masciotta. *Kokoschka*. Florence: Del Turco, 1949.

Doris Thurston. *Notes on Kokoschka*. New York: Chappaqua, 1950.

Hans M. Wingler. *Oskar Kokoschka : Orbis pictus, I & II*. Salzburg: Galerie Welz, 1951.

Paul Westheim. *Oskar Kokoschka : Gestalten und Landschaften*. Zürich: Rascher, 1952.

Hans M. Wingler. *Künstler und Poeten : Zeichnungen von Oskar Kokoschka*. Feldafing: Buchheim, 1954.

Bernhard Paumgartner. *Oskar Kokoschka : Zeichnungen für die Bühnenausstattung für W.A. Mozarts 'Zauberflöte'* (Salzburger Festspiele 1955/6). Salzburg: Galerie Welz, 1955.

Hans M. Wingler. *Oskar Kokoschka : ein Lebensbild in zeitgenössischen Dokumenten*. Munich: Albert Langen, Georg Müller, 1956.

Hans M. Wingler. *Oskar Kokoschka : das Werk des Malers*. Salzburg: Galerie Welz, 1956; tr. as *Oskar Kokoschka : the work of the painter*, London: Faber & Faber, 1958.

Hans M. Wingler. *Kokoschka-Fibel*. Salzburg: Galerie Welz, 1957; tr. as *Introduction to Kokoschka*, London: Thames and Hudson, 1958.

Bernhard Bultmann. *Oskar Kokoschka*. Salzburg: Galerie Welz, 1959; tr., London: Thames and Hudson, 1961.

Bernhard Borchert. *Kokoschka*. Berlin, 1959; tr., London: Faber & Faber, 1960.

Oskar Kokoschka : Thermopylae. Stuttgart: Reclam, 1961. introd. by Carl G. Heise; texts by Bruno Snell & the artist.

Oskar Kokoschka : watercolours, drawings, writings. London: Thames and Hudson, 1962. introd. by John Russell.

Luwig Goldscheider. *Kokoschka*. London: Phaidon, 1963. written in collaboration with the artist.

Joseph P. Hodin. *Bekenntnis zu Kokoschka : Erinnerungen und Deutungen*. Berlin, Mainz: Kupferberg, 1963.

Edgar Horstmann. *Oskar Kokoschka in Hamburg*. Hamburg: Christians, 1965.

Joseph P. Hodin. *Oskar Kokoschka : the artist and his time*. London: Cory, Adams & Mackay, 1966; tr. as *Oskar Kokoschka : sein Leben, seine Zeit*, Mainz: Kupferberg, 1968.

Fritz Schmalenbach. *Oskar Kokoschka*. Königstein im Taunus: Karl R. Langewiesche, Nachfolger Hans Koster, 1967.

Jan Tomeš. *Kokoschka : the artist in Prague*. London: Hamlyn, 1967.

Heinz Spielmann. *Oskar Kokoschka : die Fächer für Alma Mahler*. (The fans for Alma Mahler). Hamburg, 1969.

Giuseppe Gatt. *Kokoschka*. Florence: Sansoni, 1970; tr., London, New York, Sydney, Toronto, 1971.

Gerhard J. Lischka. *Oskar Kokoschka : Maler und Dichter*. Bern, Frankfurt a.M.: Peter Lang, 1972.

Jan Tomeš. *Oskar Kokoschka : Londoner Ansichten, Englische Landschaften*. Munich: Bruckmann; tr. as *Oskar Kokoschka : London views, British landscapes*, London: Thames and Hudson, 1972.

Begegnung mit Kokoschka : eine Festschrift zur Eröffnung der Oskar Kokoschka Dokumentation Pöchlarn. Pöchlarn: Oskar Kokoschka Dokumentation, 1973.

Hans M. Wingler, Friedrich Welz. *Oskar Kokoschka : das druckgraphische Werk*. Salzburg: Galerie Welz, 1975.

Ivan Fenjö. *Oskar Kokoschka : die frühe Graphik*. Vienna: Euro-Art Bücherkreis, 1976.

Oskar Kokoschka : vom Erleben im Leben, Schriften und Bilder. Salzburg: Galerie Welz, 1976. ed. by Otto Breicha.

Friedrich Welz. *Oskar Kokoschka : frühe Druckgraphik, 1906–1912*. Salzburg: Galerie Welz, 1977.

Alfred Reisinger. *Kokoschkas Dichtungen nach dem Expressionismus*. Vienna, Munich, Zürich: Europa-Verlag ('Beitrage zur österreichischen Kultur- und Geistesgeschichte', Band 2), 1978.

Hans M. Wingler, Friedrich Welz. *Oskar Kokoschka : das druckgraphische Werk II : Druckgraphik 1975–1980*. Salzburg: Galerie Welz, 1981. Supplement to 1975 catalogue raisonné.

Henry I. Schvey. *Oskar Kokoschka : the painter as playwright*. Detroit: Wayne State University Press, 1982.

Werner J. Schweiger. *Der junge Kokoschka : Leben und Werk 1904–1914*. Vienna, Munich: Christian Brandstätter, 1983.

Oskar Kokoschka : early drawings and watercolours. London: Thames and Hudson, 1985. introd. by Serge Sabarsky.

Heinz Spielmann. *Kokoschkas Fächer für Alma Mahler*. Dortmund: Die bibliophilen Taschenbücher, 1985.

Frank Whitford. *Oskar Kokoschka : a life*. London: Weidenfeld and Nicolson, 1986.